The Investigators

The Investigators

Managing FBI and Narcotics Agents

JAMES Q. WILSON

Basic Books, Inc., Publishers

New York

Library of Congress Cataloging in Publication Data

Wilson, James Q
  The investigators.

  Includes bibliographical references and index.
    1.   United States.   Federal Bureau of Investigation—
Management.   2.   United States.   Drug Enforcement
Administration—Management.   3.   Criminal investigation
—United States.   4.   Narcotics, Control of —United
States.   I.   Title.
HV8138.W633   364.12   77–20428
ISBN: 0–465–03589–2

To Diane

Intelligent management . . . must be based on exact knowledge of facts. Guesswork will not do.

JAMES J. HILL

CONTENTS

PREFACE

THIS IS A STUDY of the relationship between the tasks of federal law enforcement officers and the organizational structures within which those tasks are performed. Its objective is to assess the extent to which the management system of two important agencies—the Federal Bureau of Investigation and the Drug Enforcement Administration—facilitates or hinders the work of the investigators in those agencies and, to the extent the latter is the case, to explain why this should be so.

My motive for offering this analysis is not necessarily to make the work of the FBI or the DEA better or more rational, or to expose to public scrutiny additional problems in organizations that have, of late, been beset with controversy. Rather, it is my hope to explain how carrying out certain tasks within a governmental setting exposes managers and executives to constraints that render the devising of efficient and effective means to attain organizational objectives especially difficult or unlikely. In short, this is an account of the consequences of practicing *public* administration.

Few experienced public managers or political executives will be surprised by what follows. Lay persons, interested in obtaining better performance from government and concerned about the "bureaucracy problem," may learn something about the limits to rational behavior in a governmental, which is to say a political, setting and may come to have, in consequence, a more realistic understanding of what is possible when one attempts to supply some service under public auspices.

There were two reasons for selecting the FBI and the DEA as my examples. The first is accidental. By chance, I have been exposed to the work of these agencies over the past few years, having served officially or unofficially as a consultant to the chief administrators of each.[1] I have had an opportunity to learn at first hand about how federal investigators carry out duties that strike citizens, depending on their views, as arcane, romantic, or sinister. The second reason is, I believe, more important. The services supplied, for better or worse, by the FBI and the DEA are indisputably public or, as economists would say, collective. Whether one approves or disapproves of how the agencies behave, few would argue that they perform tasks that could as well or better be performed by private organizations. If anyone benefits from solving crimes or apprehending drug dealers, everyone benefits; thus, it would be inappropriate, except as a rather farfetched intellectual exercise, to compare the work of the FBI and the DEA with how their (imaginary) private counterparts might behave. In short, this is a study not only of public administration, but of administration that is *necessarily* public.

The time and resources necessary to begin this research were made possible by a generous subvention from National Affairs, Inc. I want to thank Irving Kristol not only for the funds, but for offering them without requiring that I do anything other than "study something you find interesting." The study could not have been completed without the grant from the Alfred P. Sloan Foundation, part of its program to stimulate at Harvard the study of public management. My thanks go to Arthur Singer and his associates at Sloan.

Clarence M. Kelley allowed me, shortly after he became director of the Federal Bureau of Investigation, to have remarkably free access to the criminal investigation units of the Bureau. John R. Bartels, Jr., and later Peter Bensinger opened the doors of the Drug Enforcement Administration to me. Dozens of administrators and agents gave generously of their time; I think it best not to name them for fear of imputing to them findings and opinions that are my own responsibility. I deeply cherish my opportunity to learn from these men.

Professor Mark H. Moore at Harvard has been a valued colleague in attempting to understand, to change, and to explain the work of federal law enforcement agencies. I have profited enormously from our many conversations and especially from his close reading of the manuscript. Philip Heymann of the Harvard Law School gave valuable advice on chapter 3. Sally Cox has typed so many manuscripts for me that I have come to take her intelligence and skill for granted. I happily acknowledge here the importance of her contribution.

The Investigators

CHAPTER

1

Bureaucracy and Law Enforcement

WHEN ONE THINKS or reads about federal agencies, one almost always thinks of the broad policies and visible personalities of the agencies. If one approves of those statements of policy or of the conduct of those personalities, one feels well disposed toward the agency, even though one would be hard pressed to say much about what the agency actually does on a day-to-day basis. If one dislikes the statements or finds the personalities unattractive, one is hostile to the agency and is inclined to grumble about the "bureaucracy problem," though without any very clear idea of what, exactly, the problem of that particular bureaucracy may be. The accounts we have of public bureaucracies are chiefly about, and sometimes by, their principal executives, and thus we learn about those personages, their fights with other high-ranking officials, and the problems they have in "getting hold of the bureaucracy." And when we add to this the interest of every president since Herbert Hoover in reorganizing, streamlining, and "reforming" the federal bureaucracy, it is hardly surprising that, as citizens, we tend to view public administration from the top down.

In the case of the Federal Bureau of Investigation and the Drug Enforcement Administration, this would seem especially appropriate. For almost half a century, the FBI and J. Edgar Hoover were virtually synonymous. It would be quite understandable if most persons, even well-informed ones, were to assume that to know what an FBI agent did it was only necessary to know what Mr. Hoover said. To an important degree this was true, as countless present and former agents will gladly or ruefully confirm. But the attention to Hoover has obscured the actual work of the Bureau and the relations—quite complex, and in significant ways unintended—between that work and Hoover's leadership.

The DEA has been involved for the last decade or so in a succession of minor scandals and personnel changes. The agency has been variously portrayed as a protector of American values and as a threat to them, as an organization of skilled professionals and as one of brutal door-smashers. It has been credited with reducing the supply of illegal drugs and blamed with allowing it (or even causing it) to increase. In all these disputes, the personality of the administrator or his immediate subordinates has been at the focus of attention. While this is quite understandable insofar as the mass media are concerned, I have found this top-down perspective also prevalent among key government officials in the White House, the Congress, and the Office of Management and Budget.

What, in my view, is missing in all this—and thus missing in a serious consideration of the "bureaucracy problem" in modern government—has been serious attention to the particular *tasks* that agencies perform. This may even be true of some business firms, though it is my impression that business executives are more likely to ask themselves the question, "what business am I really in?" than are their counterparts in government. For one thing, the success and often the remuneration of the former depends crucially on finding the right answer to that question.

The importance I attach to viewing a government agency

from the bottom up rather than from the top down may strike some readers as overstated. There seems to be nothing very mysterious about what FBI and DEA agents do— they are, after all, "cops" who work for "police" agencies by investigating crimes and arresting criminals. If they are using improper or ineffective investigative techniques, then the heads of their organizations ought to issue and enforce new instructions. If they are arresting too few or too many citizens, or arresting the wrong ones, then the top administrators should revise their guidelines for what constitutes a good or a high-priority arrest. This should be relatively easy for the executives of police agencies to do, since, as everyone knows, the police are organized along paramilitary lines with a heavy emphasis on following the chain of command and obeying orders. Naturally, there will be some slippage—not everybody will get the word and there will inevitably be a few "rotten apples" who flout the rules. But if there is a problem with the FBI or the DEA, surely it derives chiefly from bad management, poor leadership, or improper legal powers; the solution to these difficulties is to be found in Washington, where new leaders can be appointed and better laws can be passed. If, on the other hand, one believes there is nothing wrong with the FBI or the DEA that is not the result of political interference, media and congressional criticism, or insufficient funding, then, again, the solution lies primarily in Washington: leave the cops alone, end the meddling and the criticism, and appropriate more money.

The conventional view states, in brief, that it is not the tasks that are problematic, but rather the goals, resources, and leadership of the organizations in which these tasks are performed. There is just enough truth in that view, and sufficient ignorance about what FBI and DEA agents (and, I suspect, many other government employees) really do, to make it persuasive to most persons and to lead even highly placed public officials to act as if it were true.

But this top-down perspective fails to explain some important facts. During the long career of J. Edgar Hoover, when the vast majority of citizens were not only satisfied with, but enormously proud of the work of the FBI with the result that the agency was left alone and supplied with all the resources it requested, why did local United States attorneys refuse to prosecute the majority of cases presented to them by FBI agents? In 1976, the number of cases being investigated by FBI agents suddenly declined, yet the number of arrests and convictions did not. For much of its history, the number of criminal investigations the FBI had underway seemed to bear only a slight relationship to the number of arrests it managed to make.

If the top-down view can give no explanation of some facts, it can offer only an incomplete one of others. The FBI resisted for years becoming involved in organized crime and narcotics investigations. It finally capitulated on the former issue (and scored some significant victories); as late as mid-1977, it had still not yielded on the latter. A partial explanation of these positions can be found in the opinions of J. Edgar Hoover, but that is only part of the story, especially if one believes that Hoover's opposition was based on mere whim or cantankerousness.

From the early 1960s to the present, the DEA and its predecessor agencies have been the object of almost continuous controversy. Beginning in 1930 as the Federal Bureau of Narcotics, in 1968 it was taken out of the Treasury Department, merged with the Bureau of Drug Abuse Control then in the Department of Health, Education, and Welfare, and installed in the Department of Justice under a new name, the Bureau of Narcotics and Dangerous Drugs. Five years later, it was reorganized again, this time by assigning to it substantial parts of the Customs Service and all of the Office of Drug Law Enforcement and rechristening it the Drug Enforcement Administration. As this is written (mid-1977), there are rumors of yet another reorganization, perhaps involving its merger with the FBI.

In short, the DEA in the space of ten years was reorganized twice, shifted from one cabinet department to another, and led by a succession of five different administrators. Throughout this tumultuous period, however, what federal narcotics agents were doing on the street scarcely changed at all and the kind and number of arrests they made did not alter fundamentally. Of late, various critics of the DEA, notably among the staffs of key congressional committees with oversight responsibilities, have insisted that the administrators of the agency make even greater efforts to arrest fewer low-level drug dealers who are caught through "buy-and-bust" tactics on the street and more high-level traffickers who are indicted as a result of nationwide conspiracy investigations. The managers have responded by promising to do just that and have issued orders accordingly. But despite some changes in the mix of low- and high-level arrestees, the general pattern remains about the same.

This is not to say that administration makes no difference. Quite the contrary. As I hope to show, administrative systems often have a very large effect on the work of these agencies. In many cases, that effect is entirely salutary. The virtual absence of corruption among FBI agents was the result, in great part, of substantial and often ingenious administrative efforts. In other cases, however, that effect is hard to discern or even perverse—that is, administrative efforts produce either no change or the opposite of that intended. To understand why this should be so, it does little good to start at the top and inquire 'into the ability, motives, or policies of high-ranking managers, for that will only lead to the observation that sometimes agents do what is asked of them and sometimes they do not, thus implying that perhaps there is something wrong with the abilities or motives of the agents. In short, sorting out, from the top down, the effects of administrative arrangements does not solve many puzzles, it only uncovers new ones.

This book begins with a discussion of what agents do, or at

least of the important things they do with respect to criminal investigations. I do not discuss in any detail other tasks some agents perform, such as the domestic security and counterintelligence investigations carried out by the FBI and regulatory and foreign liaison work done by some DEA personnel. The reason for emphasizing criminal investigation is that this is what I could study, this task consumes the bulk of each organization's resources and of most agents' time, and this work will continue to be performed by these agencies whatever the fate of proposals to curtail or assign to other organizations counterintelligence, security, and regulatory functions.[1]

The emphasis on tasks in this study arises out of my belief that they are to an important degree the most enduring, hard-to-change elements of the situation; administrative procedures must adapt to tasks, not the other way around. The conventional view is, I think, quite different: tasks are what higher-ups in an organization say they are. Tasks are supposedly chosen, defined, revised, or discarded as a result of the efforts by administrators to achieve organizational goals or respond to public demands. I hope to show that tasks are defined by forces that are far more profound, and accordingly far more resistant to change, than the preferences of administrators. Though administrative arrangements may make it easier or harder to carry out these tasks, they rarely alter them in any serious way.

Persons with a citizen's interest in how government agencies and in particular how federal law enforcement agencies really work will have little interest in academic theories of organizational behavior. These people should skip this section and begin reading chapter 2. Here I shall try to explain how my view of organizations fits with existing theories and perspectives, not simply because such questions are of intellectual interest—though they are—but also because academic views of public administration affect, perhaps importantly, how future public administrators think of their roles and how to manage them.

The academic study of public administration operates in an intellectual atmosphere that tends to direct attention away from tasks. The reason is obvious. Scholars (as *scholars,* and not as "consultants" or "experts") are engaged in identifying and explaining uniformities in behavior. They are interested in the general, not the particular. With respect to organization and administrative behavior, their attention is drawn to those features that all or most organizations have in common, or to the systematic relationships between two aspects of organization, or to those generalizable aspects of human conduct occurring within organizations.

Only certain parts of organizations are conducive to this mode of thought. A bureaucratic organization[2] can be thought of as composed of people performing at least three essential, analytically (if not concretely) distinct functions: executives, managers, and operators. Executives are responsible for the maintenance of the organization, managers for coordinating the activities of persons within the organization, operators for performing the critical or central tasks of the organization. A "critical task" is that task the performance of which is intended to achieve the goal of the organization. Operators include doctors and nurses in a hospital, teachers in a school, patrol officers and detectives in a police department, rangers in the Forest Service, and special agents in the FBI and the DEA. From the point of view of social scientists, executives and managers are more productive objects of analysis because they perform functions that are similar in a wide variety of organizations. Hence, the executive function has been described by Barnard as involving developing goals, managing communications, and supplying incentives[3] and by Selznick as institutionalizing a distinctive competence and infusing it with value.[4] Managers have been urged by Fayol, Gulick, and Urwick to obey certain principles of management (such as "unity of command"),[5] asked by Simon to apply scientific methods in making and evaluating decisions,[6] or described by Cyert and March as responding to stress and uncertainty with "problemistic search" for satisfactory but not optimum policies.[7] Some of these analyses have been quantitative and some philosophic, some have been descriptive though most have been normative, but all have been concerned with identifying what is or ought to be *generally* true of executive and managerial functions.

Operators have been the object of studies and recommendations, but for the most part in their capacity as human beings rather than as units of organizational activity. Frederick Winslow Taylor and the disciples of "scientific management" (better named "scientific operations," since it is chiefly concerned with operators rather than managers) sought to find the "one best way" to perform various tasks, but except in its application to industries with highly routinized or mechanized technologies, this approach to organizational behavior has not been generally interesting. Indeed, worse than uninteresting, it has been unpopular and (to some) even harmful. The largest part of the vast library of studies on operators has been inspired instead by what is loosely called the "human relations" approach to organization and what in fact means the study of human interactions and satisfactions that happen to occur in organizational settings. This literature, part scholarly and part evangelical, has succeeded in casting doubt on Taylorian assumptions about the adaptability and rationality of operators (though it has not as yet shown what some of its early advocates claimed, namely, that in every organization benevolent management, democratic procedures, and a lessening in power differences will lead simultaneously to greater happiness and more productivity).

The hard fact is that the tasks that organizational operators perform are so numerous and diverse as to defy—so far, and perhaps always—systematic classification and generalization. Executives or managers may perform similar functions in a variety of organizations, but operators tend to perform different operations in different organizations. There have been sophisticated attempts to analyze in general terms classes of tasks or technologies in organizations, but the classifications are of necessity so abstract as to be of interest only to persons concerned with the most general properties of organizations.[8]

Because what organizations actually do—which is to say, how their central tasks are defined and executed—is so obviously important to citizens and clients, it was only a matter of time before scholars became interested in this aspect of their behavior. Economists have always been interested in the outputs of organizations, though rarely in the internal arrangements that are responsible for those outputs. Students of public administration are coming to share that interest, often describing it as the analysis of "service delivery." Initially, much of that analysis was based on the assumption that the important differences in outputs or services could be explained by the nature of the recipient of those services —his or her race, class, age, neighborhood, or political power.[9] Gradually it became clear that it was the internal procedures of the agency itself, more than the attributes of its clients, that accounted for most of the variance in outputs. Though different political systems no doubt produce different levels of various public services, explaining that difference, and certainly explaining what can be observed in a single jurisdiction, requires close attention to how the agency defines and manages its tasks.

The actual, day-to-day tasks of a public agency are rarely of much interest to scholars, however, in part because they are difficult to study (one must observe human behavior rather than merely interview "respondents" or analyze available statistics), but in greater part because the number and variety of organizational tasks defy generalization. Interesting books have been written about the work of forest rangers,[10] police officers,[11] prison guards,[12] diplomats,[13] state employment officers, and federal wage and hour inspectors,[14] but nobody has tried—or at least tried very seriously—to make any general statements about what the work of these various occupations has in common, or how systematic differences in this work are associated with interesting and systematic differences in organizational processes. Scholars have an interest in uniformities and systematic variations; they tend to shun subjects that seem relentlessly unique, idiosyncratic, or random.

If one cannot generalize about tasks, what intellectual value is there in studying them? The answer, I think, is that though tasks seem infinitely various, critical tasks tend to persist. They are refractory. Operators performing them resist change and even intrusion, and struggle to assert their autonomy over how tasks are carried out. Persons performing different tasks often do not work well together, unless each operation can be made relatively independent of the other.

The fact that organizations are resistant to change is well known—perhaps too well known, for what is striking about the bureaus and agencies of official Washington is not how stable they are, but how often they are shuffled around. Tasks, however, are harder to change than organizations. More exactly, what operators do in an organization is harder to alter than the formal relationships that exist among groups of operators, or among managers that supervise the operators, or among different organizational units. This fact (if, as I think, it *is* a fact) helps explain why government reorganizations can occur so often without any discernible change in the way a governmental employee actually performs his or her work. Bureaus are reorganized, cabinet secretaries and agency heads come and go, new departments are created or merged, and yet, to the citizen-client, little seems to change.

The ways in which tasks get defined and the mechanisms that enable them to resist change will be discussed in chapter 7. For now, it is important to remember that bureaucracies, public and private, go to considerable lengths to create a set of attitudes or an organizational ethos that will lead members to resist change, and in many ways the best bureaucracies are those most successful at instilling this ethos. This seems paradoxical: why should the administrator of an organization, who wants his operators to follow orders, including orders to change their ways of doing things, devote any effort to cultivating attitudes that will reinforce the operators' resistance to change?

The answer, I believe, is that organizations are easier and more economical to manage when there is a strong belief among operators in the rightness of their tasks. By "economical," I mean requiring less of an executive's supply of scarce incentives. By "easier," I mean requiring less information, fewer instructions, and less exacting supervision. Most organizations try to develop a sense of what has been variously called "mission," "essence," or "distinctive competence."[15] I will use these terms interchangeably to refer to a widely shared view among organization members as to the nature, feasibility, and importance of the organization's principal tasks, or some significant portion of these tasks. Very few organizations, if any, are so fortunate as to have only tasks that are part of its mission. In almost every case, members of the organization distinguish between the "real work" of the organization (selling insurance, flying bombers, making arrests, caring for patients) and the "garbage work" (filling out forms, obtaining supplies, dealing with disputes, handling complaints). Many organizations have two or more missions: in the Navy, submarine patrol and aircraft-carrier task forces; in the Air Force, manning strategic bombers, operating missiles, and flying tactical aircraft. Since a sense of mission becomes the basis for organizational loyalty, having two or more missions becomes the basis for organizational conflict.

Strong organizations are typically those in which the sense of mission is widely shared and successfully adapted to the requirements of organizational survival and enhancement.[16]

We describe such organizations as having a high *ésprit de corps*, but we sometimes fail to note that this implies more than mere high morale or good feelings; it refers to an attachment to a distinctive way of doing things. The greater that attachment, the easier it is to manage the organization in the performance of its tasks. Management involves coordinating human behavior, which in turn means getting two or more people to act in the same way or toward common objectives. If the right way of doing the "real" work of the organization is widely shared and highly valued, then the level of detailed and particular supervision need not be as great as when the tasks are "just a job."

A sense of mission becomes the basis, explicitly or implicitly, on which personnel are recruited, trained, rewarded, and managed. Philip Selznick, from whom my views on this matter are so obviously derived, has remarked that an organizational mission is not simply the formal goal of the organization but the distinctive *and valued* set of behaviors, selected from among a large number of behaviors, by which activity toward a goal and organizational maintenance are reconciled. Mission, in short, implies much more than the neutral, technical term, "means."

Business firms display an awareness of their critical tasks on pain of failure. Paul Lawrence and Jay Lorsch observed that firms selling plastics, containers, and packaged foods all had the same goal—making money—and employed essentially the same means—design, manufacturing, marketing— but each had, as a result of the nature of its business environment, a quite different problem to solve and thus task to perform. Plastics firms had to adapt to rapidly changing technology and consumer demand by conceiving and inventing new products; price was less important than anticipation and imagination. Container firms, on the other hand, provided standardized product to a stable, predictable market; the key problem was to control costs and manage inventories. The food manufacturers had to innovate so as to anticipate (or create) demand, but in the context of a stable technology and keen price competition. In each organization that was successful, a distinctive structure emerged ("tall" or "flat," rigid or flexible) and power and status went to those who performed the critical tasks—in plastics to the product designers and inventors, but in containers to the cost accountants and schedulers.[17]

Government agencies cannot so readily adapt to the requirements of their critical tasks because their structure and resources are determined, in large measure, by forces (legislators, elected executives) outside their control and in part because such agencies must, by virtue of being public, serve many goals in addition to (and often in conflict with) their mission—political accountability, openness to scrutiny, a civil service personnel system, and so forth. The political process may assure their survival without requiring them to meet a market test, but at a heavy price in constraints and conflicts.

In the firms studied by Lawrence and Lorsch, it was clear that—at least in the successful businesses—the key tasks importantly affected the way the organization was designed and run. For the FBI and the DEA, and perhaps for many other government agencies, operator tasks do not strongly shape managerial strategies. In consequence of this, tensions between operators and managers, between "the field" and "headquarters," are especially acute.

In what follows, these issues will be examined by looking in turn at each distinctive role in the two organizations—the operators (chapter 2), the managers (chapters 4 and 5), and the executives (chapter 6). I stress that this is not a comparative evaluation of the two agencies. Each has strengths and weaknesses. Each, in my view, is necessary; neither can be a model for the other. FBI and DEA agents often speak critically of each other's organization; this account is not a reckoning up of the score. Nor is this study an evaluation of the effectiveness of these agencies in combating crime or narcotics trafficking. To do that would require an analysis of crime (since law enforcement is only one factor that influences the rate at which crime occurs) and of the drug problem in its international as well as domestic aspects. This is, rather, an effort to explain how two important federal agencies are routinely managed; and it is written in the belief that an understanding of what governments ordinarily do is among the surest revelations of the essential nature of government itself.

CHAPTER

2

Investigators

TRADITIONALLY, the criminal investigator—popularly, the detective—has been thought of as embodying the essence of law enforcement: solving crimes by shrewd deduction, scientific inquiry, and artful surmise. The uniformed patrol officer may respond first to a victim's call and on occasion might catch the thief in the act, but generally his task, or so it was thought, was to secure the crime scene, calm the victim, fill out routine forms, and call the detectives. These investigators, in plainclothes and unmarked cars, would then set to work on the arduous task of tracking down the culprit.

Recent research has cast doubt on this view. A substantial body of evidence gathered in many different cities strongly suggests that investigators actually account for only a small portion of the arrests of even the most serious criminals and that even these few are caught not because of the detectives' skill at logical inference, scientific inquiry, or investigative techniques, but because a victim or witness has already supplied a positive identification of the suspect. In a study of arrest records for serious crimes in five cities, Peter W. Greenwood and his colleagues at RAND found that two thirds of the sample of 172 arrests were made because of an initial identification of the suspect by patrolmen, victims, or witnesses, and that of those arrests made despite the absence of an initial positive identification, most resulted from quite routine work, primarily involving witness examination of photographs ("mug shots") of possible suspects or from happenstance (as when a victim later spotted the culprit or a person arrested on another charge was found to have in his possession stolen property from the initial crime).[1] A study by the Police Foundation of arrest records in three large cities revealed that about two thirds of the arrests for serious, stranger-to-stranger crimes were made by uniformed patrol officers, often because they caught the perpetrator in the act or because they were able to give chase soon after the crime occurred.[2] In both the RAND and Police Foundation studies, detectives, relying on their own resources, accounted for only between 3 and 12 percent of the arrests.

The Federal Bureau of Investigation and the Drug Enforcement Administration are composed, at the operating level, almost exclusively of investigators. Neither agency performs any patrol functions. Each is charged with solving major crimes—violations of the federal criminal code (some of which, such as bank robbery and kidnapping, carry heavy penalties) and of the Comprehensive Drug Abuse Prevention and Control Act. If investigators, as they function within city police departments, play such a small role in arresting serious offenders, of what value are those assigned to federal law enforcement agencies? What do detectives *do?* Imagine, for example, that you are told to solve a bank robbery or a theft from an interstate shipment—where would you begin? How would you spend your day? What technologies, if any, would you employ?

The answers to such questions are not important merely because they satisfy our curiosity but also because they help explain the problem of managing and maintaining an investigative organization. Patrol officers, for example, make most of the arrests in a police department, but this behavior—arresting—is not the essence of their task and does not decisively shape the occupational and organizational milieu in which they work. This is true not only because the patrol officer spends relatively little of his time making important arrests, but also because the other things he does give rise to his most important problems.

As I have written elsewhere, the "patrolman's role is defined more by his responsibility for *maintaining* order than by his responsibility for enforcing the law."[3] To maintain order he must cope with disorder that arises out of disputes over what is right and seemly conduct or out of disputes over who is to blame for conduct that is agreed to be wrong or unseemly. The patrol officer must impose standards of proper conduct on people who may not share those standards, and he must often do so in a tense, violent, or emotional situation: the family fight, the streetcorner brawl, the raucous juvenile crowd. The law places constraints on what the officer can do in these circumstances and offers him (or her) one method, an arrest, for managing them, but the constraints are rarely so precise as to define a single correct solution to the problem, and the arrest is often not an appropriate remedy. The officer must somehow "handle the situation." People will disagree as to whether he has handled it properly, and his superiors will often have little information about how he has handled it at all. As a result, the officer often finds himself in difficult situations with no guidance as to how he ought to behave, and the police manager or executive often lacks timely information with which to guide and evaluate the officers under his command.

Presumably, the investigator suffers from none of these difficulties. He rarely must maintain order, for he does not answer every citizen call for assistance, only those prompted by the commission of a serious crime, usually occurring some time before the call is placed. He has what would appear to be a clear performance standard: solving the crime, usually by making arrests. His superiors have (in theory, at least) an unambiguous criterion by which to evaluate his performance: the proportion of crimes on which he works that he solves. And the community does not confront the detective or his superiors with conflicting values—while citizens will disagree as to what constitutes right and seemly conduct, they will usually agree that murder, robbery, burglary, and illicit trafficking in dangerous drugs are wrong, that they are worthwhile objects for investigatory efforts, and that those responsible for these offenses deserve punishment.

In fact, the task of the investigator, though clearly different from that of the patrol officer, is itself subject to important difficulties that make the management of an investigatory agency, though different from that of a patrol one, a complex and often frustrating problem. One of these difficulties has already been described. Much investigation depends on luck—on whether the victim reports the crime (especially rare in narcotics cases but far from the universal practice even for ordinary crimes), on whether the victim or witness is willing and able to identify and testify against the suspect, and on whether an unknown or elusive suspect will later be caught under incriminating circumstances so that his earlier offense can be solved. In addition, a detective works under far clearer and more confining legal constraints than a patrol officer. The latter can devise informal remedies for disorderly situations and impose "curbstone justice" for many minor legal infractions. These decisions are rarely reviewed—because they are rarely known—by higher authorities. Even when the patrol officer makes a major arrest, it is typically under circumstances—such as catching a thief or assaulter in the act—that make it unlikely that prosecution will be blocked by legal objections to the quality of the evidence. An investigator, on the other hand, because he often makes arrests some time after the crime was committed and on the basis of a *belief* (rather than the certain knowledge) that the suspect is the guilty party, must worry whether his arrest will be sustained and his evidence admitted in court.

Finally, certain kinds of investigation are not intended to lead to arrests and court cases. Counterespionage and political security investigations may have as their object the surreptitious disruption of clandestine or ideological organizations. An arrest, far from being the goal, might even be a mark of failure because it would, for example, prematurely alert the opposition to one's surveillance or make the public at large aware that disruptive activities are occurring of which they might disapprove. And even when, as in a narcotics or organized crime investigation, an arrest is a desired outcome, it is not the only one; arresting two or three gamblers or drug dealers might be less important than dismantling or crippling the criminal organization itself.

Types of Investigation

Investigative activities are of several sorts, depending on the amount of information one has about the crime (or, as in security cases, about the status of the subject or organization) and the degree of control one can exercise over the suspect(s). There are four possibilities.

In the first, a suspect has been apprehended or a subject placed under control and there is adequate information about the person's behavior—if a criminal, the information is adequate to make an arrest; if an informant or spy, the investigator has adequate and reliable information about the subject's conduct. In criminal matters of this kind, there is no investigatory problem, only one of prosecution or case management. No further reference will be made to this situation.

In the second case, there is reliable information that a crime has been committed, but the suspect has not been identified or, if identified, not apprehended. For example, a bank was robbed, but the police do not know who did it or, if they do know, they cannot locate him. This is the classic problem of *detection:* to discover reliable information that will permit the identification and arrest of a perpetrator.

In the third case, a suspect or subject may be known or even under continuous observation or control, but there is no reliable or adequate information about this person's past behavior, present connections, or future intentions. This could occur when, for example, a low-level drug dealer is identified in whom the police have little interest other than as a means to discover other as yet unknown persons who supply the dealer or who are his customers. This case is to be distinguished from the preceding one by noting that the investigators are not reacting to the fact that a crime has been committed but are hoping to discover a crime that can implicate a targeted individual or his confederates. Such investigations may involve following a suspect or making him the object of electronic surveillance, or they may involve efforts to encourage the commission of a crime in which the suspect will participate while under observation. This is the interesting and distinctive case, and will be referred to as the problem of *instigation;* officers who do this work will be referred to as instigative, as opposed to investigative, agents. (The term "instigator" should not be misunderstood. I do not mean that instigators practice entrapment by inducing a person to commit a crime he would otherwise not commit, though, if instigators misuse their powers, that can occur. "Instigator" is a legally neutral term referring to a law enforcement officer who, by assuming the role of a criminal, provides an opportunity to commit a consensual crime for a person who is ready, willing, and seeking an opportunity to do so.)

The final case involves the absence of both an identified subject and adequate information. Nonetheless, there are reasons, ranging from a hunch to the tips of untested informants to the implications of other investigative reports, that "something may be up" or something bears watching. An exploratory inquiry is made by analyzing available information, looking for hitherto unknown relationships among known subjects, randomly investigating locales or situations, or canvassing informants for tips on new activities. This is *intelligence* work, much but not all of which may be performed by people who never leave their offices and who usually are not thought of as investigators at all. Indeed, as will be discussed in chapter 5, the failure of intelligence specialists to be actively involved in detection or instigation—their failure, in short, to be "on the street"—creates formidable barriers to their effective communication with detectives and instigators. And this leads to their being ignored even when they have useful information, or to their failing to know what information might be useful. ("Intelligence" as used here refers to an occupation or role, not to a type of case. In the FBI, intelligence means investigative work directed at persons, organizations, or nations threatening the peace and security of the United States. Intelligence work in that sense can be carried on by detectives, instigators, or intelligence specialists.)

FBI Agents as Detectives

Agents (technically, "special agents") of the Federal Bureau of Investigation, insofar as they function as detectives, are chiefly concerned with the purposeful gathering and recording of information in order to present a case for prosecution. The test of success is whether the prosecutor—almost always a local United States attorney or one of his assistants—will accept the case and this, in turn, depends on the laws governing standards of proof and the admissibility of evidence as well as on the prosecutor's view as to what constitutes an important or worthwhile case. In short, detectives are chiefly interviewers who work, in fact if not in law, for a client who announces in advance the kind of information he requires.

In a typical FBI field office, most special agents do detective work. In one, 109 special agents worked as investigators:[4] 61 worked almost entirely as detectives and 48 on assignments involving primarily intelligence and instigative work. The 61 detectives were organized into six squads of about 10 agents each: the "ASAC's Squad," concerned primarily with bank robberies; the C-1 squad, concerned mostly with interstate auto thefts; the C-2 squad, concerned with theft of government property, crimes on government reservations (such as military bases or veterans' hospitals), and copyright violations; the C-4 squad, devoted to locating fugitives from justice and to conducting background checks on persons who had applied for jobs with the Bureau or elsewhere in the Department of Justice; the C-5 squad, concerned with fraud, especially in banks, and with other so-called "white-collar" crimes; and the C-6 squad, concerned with thefts from interstate shipments and the interstate transportation of stolen property.

Some members of the other squads also do detective work, but often they are concerned with matters in which no crime has been reported. The C-3 squad is preoccupied with organized crime cases, primarily those involving leading members of what the Bureau has called "LCN." ("La Cosa Nostra" is its term, acquired from the testimony of Joseph Valachi, for what everybody else calls the Mafia or the Syndicate.) There were then also three squads (S-1, S-2, and S-3) concerned with security matters, chiefly domestic political security (what the Bureau once called "extremist matters") and foreign espionage, as well as with violations of various civil rights acts. When there are many civil rights matters, as was the case in Boston during 1974–75 owing to the tumult surrounding the court-ordered busing of pupils in order to integrate the public schools, agents assigned to the squad (S-3) handling such matters found themselves doing detective work—gathering information for the possible prosecution of those who had violated the civil rights of others. In ordinary times, this squad does intelligence work.

Unlike the cases handled by the detectives of a city police force, those that make up the bulk of an FBI agent's workload come not from individuals but from other organizations. Occasionally a citizen will call the FBI to report a crime, and sometimes, as with kidnappings, they are serious ones, but for the most part FBI cases come from business firms, other government agencies, state and local police departments, or from other offices of the FBI that request the local office to check out a lead from a case in another city. The reason for the relative scarcity of individual complainants is that, in almost every criminal matter, the FBI shares jurisdiction with local police authorities, and it is to these authorities that citizens first turn when they have been raped, assaulted, robbed, burgled, or had their cars stolen. Most of these common crimes involve no federal violation, so the FBI never hears of them except statistically. And even when a common form of individual victimization, such as auto theft, involves a federal violation because the stolen car was driven across a state line, it is not the victimized owner who calls the FBI but rather the local police agency that has recovered the car.

In consequence of handling primarily *organizational* complaints, FBI agents rarely have to witness or cope with disorder, rarely need to interview a distraught or injured victim, and rarely need to give chase to a fleeing suspect. Sometimes a suspect they have identified will, when faced with the prospect of arrest, put up a fight, and of course FBI agents have been killed in the line of duty, but this is comparatively infrequent. Since the Bureau was founded in 1924, only about two dozen special agents have died from

criminal assaults. For city police officers, the need to manage disorder and to give chase to suspects creates a constant
threat of violence that powerfully conditions their attitudes
and behavior.[5] Between 1965 and 1974, nearly a thousand
police officers were killed feloniously, mostly by firearms.[6]

Because the FBI agent is ordinarily dealing with a calm
complainant (often an organizational representative who was
not personally victimized) who reports a crime several days,
perhaps weeks, old, the agent is less preoccupied than a city
patrol officer or detective with finding ways of successfully
asserting his authority over tense, frightened, quarrelsome,
or hostile persons. Or more accurately: given the situation in
which most FBI interviews take place, the agent can rely,
much more than a city police officer, on his office and legal
powers as a source of authority and much less on his personal manner, masculinity, or shrewd street sense.

J. Edgar Hoover created a legend—and a source of much
good-natured joking—when he insisted that FBI agents
wear conservative, businesslike clothes and conduct themselves in an orderly, conventional manner. Given the task of
the FBI agent acting as a detective, this was a sound and
feasible strategy: sound because it emphasized the reliance
on formal rather than personal sources of authority in ways
that built public confidence in the agents and feasible because the situations with which the agents had to cope were
not ordinarily ones that required displays of personal dominance, physical strength, or identification with the victims.

The fact that FBI agents, in their detective capacity, carry
out investigations of serious but almost always nonviolent
offenses reported to them by organizations some time
—often a considerable time—after the crime occurred
means that an agent's behavior can more easily be made subject to rules and discipline. The agent is not in hot pursuit of
a fleeing suspect, nor is he likely to encounter the suspect
still at the scene of the crime (as many police officers do
when they investigate shootings and assaults among friends

and relatives). He rarely, therefore, is called upon to arrest somebody because he *thinks* the person committed the crime—technically, because he has "probable cause" to believe that a felony occurred and that the person in view committed it—but only when he has satisfied himself, an assistant United States attorney, and a federal magistrate that an arrest is in order. He has, in short, time to build a case. As a result, the great majority of arrests made by an FBI agent are made by executing an arrest warrant issued by a judicial officer. An agent is legally empowered to make an arrest without a warrant if an offense against federal laws is committed in his presence or if he has "reasonable grounds" for believing that a person "committed or is committing" a federal felony. In fact, this authority is rarely exercised. Indeed, the *FBI Handbook* instructs agents that, "wherever possible, prosecution should be authorized and a warrant issued prior to an arrest." An arrest without a warrant is acceptable only in "emergency situations."

There are three major exceptions to this state of affairs. When a bank is robbed, the FBI responds immediately. Occasionally agents arrive when the robbers are still inside or visibly in flight. The FBI must help apprehend the suspects in these cases just as if they were local police officers, but often the charging and prosecution of these cases is turned over to the local police who will also be on the scene. The "locals" usually will have to handle whatever evidentiary problems may result. A second exception is when a crime, especially one of violence, occurs on a government reservation, such as in a hospital run by the Veterans Administration. On government reservations, the FBI has jurisdiction over ordinary criminal matters and hence must function precisely as if it were a city detective squad. Many agents speak distastefully of this work, perhaps because it is unfamiliar (it is a rare agent who has to investigate a murder, assault, or rape, and thus when one happens, the agent assigned may be unprepared for it) and perhaps also because it involves dealing with many petty offenses and not a few victims who were involved in complex and unsatisfactory ways with their assailants. Routine violent crime does not often present the investigator with a wholly innocent victim, an entirely disinterested witness, and a completely culpable suspect. The third exception, rare in the past but more common in recent years, occurs when imminent and lethal violence is threatened in a place or by persons over whom the FBI has jurisdiction—an aircraft hijacking, a bomb threat in a federal building, or snipers on an Indian reservation. The FBI has had to develop special procedures to handle these incidents, and their occurrence causes considerable anxiety among Bureau executives, but they remain (except for bomb scares) relatively uncommon occurrences.

The orderly manner in which most cases arise means that, within limits, FBI agents can control their own working hours. Whereas a city police detective squadroom will usually have someone present around the clock and on weekends, with the investigators handling homicides and assaults putting in a great deal of night work, and whereas the offices of a narcotics enforcement squad will start to come alive at night as agents get ready to go out and make buys on the street, FBI agents work daylight hours, Monday through Friday. A night supervisor will be on duty to handle any incoming calls and, if necessary, call out an agent after hours or on weekends, but generally a Bureau field office is quiet outside regular working hours. (These, it should be noted, are not exactly banker's hours: owing to the agents' desire for overtime pay and the organization's policy of "expecting" overtime work, agents typically begin at 7 A.M. and work to 6 P.M. or later.) Except for the problem of geographical reassignment, something that is common only for new agents or those aspiring to higher administrative posts, an FBI agent can count on leading something approaching a normal family life—as normal, that is, as is permitted by one's neighbors' realization that one *is* an FBI agent.

The fact that FBI criminal jurisdiction is shared with state and local police means that, within the limits imposed by Bureau and United States attorney policy, the agents working as detectives can manage at the margin their own workload. A city police department must make some response to every citizen call and complainant; in most cases, that response is nothing more than the taking of a report by a patrol officer. City detectives may make only perfunctory efforts to "solve" crimes—they know better than anyone that there is little they can do to make an arrest when the victim or witness has not himself provided the essential information. But because the police have general and original jurisdiction over all crimes committed in their community and because they are a local agency held responsible, however uncertainly, for local crime conditions, any crime reported to them becomes *their* crime and any failure to solve it counts against them. The FBI is not in this position. When the United States attorney agrees, it can and does decline to pursue many matters on the grounds that it is a purely local affair, and even when there is a clear violation of a federal statute the Bureau can decline to make a serious inquiry. An FBI agent's workload, therefore, is not determined by objective circumstances over which he has no control, such as the number of crimes reported to the Bureau by citizens, but by organizational policies and the incentives operating on the agent. His workload consists of those cases that Bureau policy requires him to accept or those cases that, within Bureau guidelines, he has chosen to accept.

How much discretion an agent or a field office should have in making these judgments has been, as will be shown in chapter 5, a matter of deep and persistent debate within the Bureau, but that discretion can be used to set the workload is beyond dispute. For example, from December 1973 to January 1976, the number of pending matters in the workload of one FBI field office fell from 6,733 to 4,241 despite the fact that crime rates were going up. This resulted not from a field office desire to ignore crime but from a policy that enabled it to drop from its caseload a large number of matters that to it, and probably to any observer, were trivial. The controllable nature of the workload means that, again as will be discussed in chapter 5, any statistical measure of efficiency or productivity, such as a "crime clearance" or "conviction" ratio, may be quite suspect: the denominator of that ratio, as well as the numerator, is affected by organizational policy.

Some of the decisions as to what FBI agents will investigate are made not by the agent or the Bureau but by the local United States attorney and sometimes (given its authority in this matter, surprisingly rarely) by the Department of Justice, which nominally supervises both the FBI and United States attorneys (USAs). Though any stolen car transported across a state line constitutes a violation of the Dyer Act,[7] the Department of Justice decided in 1970 not to prosecute interstate auto-theft cases where the guilty person was under the age of twenty-one and not a serious recidivist or over the age of twenty-one and not previously convicted of a felony, unless the car was one of several cars stolen by a "car ring," was stripped or demolished, or was used to commit a separate felony.[8] Many local USAs apply this even more narrowly: they will not accept any "single car" cases whatever the identity of the suspect; they only want to prosecute "ring" cases. Federal statute also places limits on Bureau jurisdiction. Only if stolen goods that are moved in interstate commerce are valued at $5,000 or more does the thief violate *federal* law.[9] But this limit is not a helpful investigatory guideline, for only after the case is solved can one know for certain whether something stolen worth over $5,000 did or did not cross a state line. How, then, is the Bureau to decide whether to look into the matter in the first place? The *FBI Handbook*, reflecting Department of Justice policy, instructs agents to investigate automatically all thefts involving $50,000 or more, assuming that the goods will enter interstate commerce, but to investigate thefts of more than $5,000 but less than $50,000 only if there is a "reasonable inference" that the property crossed a state line.

Some guidelines are imposed by USAs without any Justice Department or statutory authorization at all. One federal prosecutor announced that his office would decline to prosecute as felonies any thefts from interstate shipments where goods valued at less than $2,000 were taken and would decline to prosecute as misdemeanors such thefts where less than $500 was taken. (The statute puts no value minima on such thefts; *all* are, strictly speaking, illegal.[10])

In general, FBI agents are pleased to have clear guidelines because it helps them avoid wasting time on cases without prosecutive potential, but they worry about letting persons who have broken the law get away with it just because they were lucky or clever enough to steal amounts below the USA's minimum. Technically, of course, local police and prosecutors may proceed with cases that fall below federal standards, but in fact these agencies are also overburdened and, in addition, frequently lack the resources with which to develop an interstate case. It takes money to send investigators to interview out-of-state witnesses or to bring such witnesses back to the local jurisdiction so that they might testify in court. As one assistant United States attorney put it to an interviewer, "the locals won't touch these cases, especially if the witness is from out of state. I sympathize with the FBI; a lot of people are getting a free ride."

Working a Case

When a case arrives at an FBI field office, it is recorded on a complaint form and assigned by the group supervisor in charge of cases of that type to one of his agents. That agent then "has the ticket" on that case, and responsibility for its management and for meeting reporting requirements about it thereafter rests squarely on his shoulders. The agent will routinely have the "indices" (a card-file system on which is indexed information from past case files) checked to see what he can learn about the victim, the suspect ("subject," in Bureau language) if known, and any other significant features of the case. A "rotor clerk" will then open a file on this new case and assign it a serial number; while the case is being worked, it is kept in a rotary file in the agent's group. *Everything* pertaining to the case is typed up by Bureau stenographers and filed; a copy of these materials is charged out by the agent and kept in his "work box," consisting of all pending matters assigned to him. Every night he must lock up his work box in a safe. When the case is closed, the files leave the agent and the rotor clerk and go to the permanent serial files in the field office. Another file is kept at FBI headquarters but this will contain copies of only a portion of the materials gathered in the field.

If the case has a subject—as when a witness has identified a person who may have committed the crime—an "agency check" is run, usually by a clerk specially trained for this job. Various local police departments are called, as are the state police, the state department of motor vehicles, the probation and parole offices, and any other government organization that might have useful information about the subject. If the case has an unknown subject (in Bureau language, it is an "unsub"), the investigative task becomes infinitely more difficult—often, impossible.

There are scores of criminal matters over which the FBI exercises jurisdiction and about which it keeps separate statistics. In January 1976, one field office had in these categories about 2,000 active criminal cases pending, most of which had been assigned to a case agent. A few major categories, however, account for the bulk of these matters and for almost all of the serious ones. Six—theft from interstate shipment (TFIS), interstate transportation of stolen motor vehicles (ITSMV), bank fraud, interstate transportation of stolen property (ITSP), fugitives ("unauthorized flight to avoid prosecution," or UFAP), and bank robbery—accounted for 994, or almost half of all pending criminal matters. In addition, there were over 500 leads on criminal cases from other field offices that had to be checked out and reported on.

Every agent informally classifies each case as promising or unpromising on the basis of several criteria. The most important of these is whether or not he thinks he can solve it, and that, in turn, depends more than anything else on whether he has a subject or a good lead on a subject. One agent told an interviewer in 1974 that of the 36 theft cases in his active file, only 9 had subjects (that is, suspects) and the rest were "unsub." Most of his known subject cases he regarded as promising, though some were minor offenses in which he would invest effort only to satisfy statistical requirements. Few of the unsub cases were deemed promising, except for two: in one, the theft was so large (some valuable paintings had been stolen) that he planned to keep working on it in the hope that something would break; in the other, also a large theft, there was physical evidence that might prove useful.

The nature of the offense importantly affects the probability of having a known subject. Subjects are most likely to be identified when there are eyewitnesses (as with amateur bank robberies, bribery cases, and assaults on government reservations), when the opportunity to commit the offense is limited to one or a small number of persons (as with bank fraud and embezzlement), or when identifiable stolen property is resold or offered to an innocent buyer (as with auto-theft rings, forged or bad check cases, copyright violations, or stolen securities). They are least likely to be identified when a crime of stealth is committed not involving the resale of the loot (as with the stealing of cash from an office or armored car), when the property stolen is not identifiable (as with the hijacking of cigarettes or liquor from an interstate shipment), or when the crime occurs before witnesses but the perpetrators are well disguised (as with the more professional bank robberies).

This difference in the likelihood of a case producing a subject has important consequences for the conviction rates. Except for bank robbery, the FBI does not calculate solution or conviction rates, but a crude approximation can be obtained by dividing the number of cases under investigation for a given offense into the number of convictions for that offense. In January 1975, there were pending in one field office 551 matters involving crimes that are likely to produce subjects: auto theft, copyright violations, bank or government fraud, and bribery. During fiscal 1975, there were in the local federal court 85 convictions of persons charged with these offenses, or a "conviction rate" of 15.4 percent. At the same time, there were under investigation 611 matters involving crimes less likely to produce subjects: theft from interstate shipment or of government property and interstate transportation of stolen property. Only 46 convictions resulted from these investigations, for a rate of 7.5 percent. Crimes with a high probability of producing "subs" were twice as likely to result in convictions as those with a high probability of being "unsub."

If there is a subject, the agent's job is primarily to develop confirming evidence and to locate and apprehend the person. This involves chiefly interviewing witnesses, associates, and acquaintances of the subject, and often the suspect himself in the hope of eliciting a confession. If there is no subject but if on other grounds the case seems important, then the agent must either "hope for a break" (for example, a person arrested for another crime confesses to the federal violation also or recovered stolen goods can be traced back to the thief) or he must develop an informant.

The informant is a crucial investigatory resource. In February 1976, I interviewed ten FBI agents who were investigating a total of 86 criminal matters, 26 of which were leads that were being serviced for another field office. Of the 60 matters for which their field office was the "office of origin," about half involved the use of an informant. These cases included auto theft, bank robbery, burglary, organized prostitution, loansharking, gambling, bank embezzlement, thefts from interstate shipments, stolen checks, stolen securities, and fugitives. In the 20 cases in which an arrest had been made or was imminent, 13 involved the important use of an informant or a cooperating defendant. In some cases, the informant was used purely for purposes of detection, as when an underworld figure tipped off the FBI as to what gang had committed a bank robbery. In other cases, a cooperating individual was used to gather direct evidence, as when the victim of a loanshark allowed the FBI to conceal on his person a miniature tape recorder (a "consensual body recorder") while he did business with the illegal lender. And in still other cases, the informant may be used for instigative rather than detective purposes, as when an informant, after being approached by thieves, helped set up a potential hijacking of a truck while FBI agents watched, ready to make an arrest (the hijacking gang was "spooked"—became suspicious and abandoned the act—and no arrests resulted).

The development and use of informants is so important an aspect of detective work that an extensive discussion of it will be found in chapter 3. It is important to stress here, however, that the ability to develop an informant is a vital investigatory skill, and one at which not all agents are equally adept. Indeed, informant management may be even more important for FBI agents than for most detectives because the former only rarely work undercover. Many city detectives, and most narcotics agents, will spend a great deal of their time impersonating criminals, fences, or "street people"; with a few exceptions, and those chiefly to be found in the security field, FBI agents work overtly. Hoover did not like undercover operations and of course the dress code of the agents would have made it ludicrous for most of them to even attempt to go undercover—there are not many hijackers or auto thieves who could easily be impersonated by short-haired, clean-shaven agents. Even with the liberalized dress code in the modern Bureau, there are still relatively few agents whose appearance is well suited to going undercover.

Whether developing an informant, speaking to a victim or witness, or canvassing the neighborhood of a crime, the essential task and critical skill of the detective is his ability to conduct a productive interview. In this, the detective's craft is not unlike that of the newspaper reporter, albeit it is practiced under different legal constraints and with different outcomes. Detectives, like reporters, are expected always to identify themselves, to take full and accurate notes, to get all the essential details, and to have a flair for inducing worried or suspicious people to trust them or at least to tell them more than they intend. And they must alike have the judgment to distinguish the statements of persons who are self-aggrandizing, unreliable, or gossip-mongers from those of subjects who are candid, detached, and factual. As one veteran (and by his colleagues, revered) FBI agent told an interviewer, "Talking to people is the name of the game; everything else is just overhead." His interviewing abilities were legendary—he had persuaded corrupt public officials, dishonest businessmen, and major organized crime figures to open up to him. He had little patience with those who shunned the street, devoted themselves to paperwork, or were ambitious for higher administrative positions: "Some of these guys don't know their ass because they are the ones who want to get away from real investigative work."

Most interviewing is quite prosaic, even tedious. One agent I accompanied spent much of his afternoon trying to locate a bartender who was on duty at a local motel when a person suspected of committing a major theft was supposedly drinking at the bar and conferring with a confederate. If the bartender could be found and could remember the suspect, his evidence might help support the allegation that the suspect was in the city at the time of the crime; with luck, the bartender might even have overheard the conversation. Unfortunately, the bartender remembered nothing. Another agent interviewed a family that had accepted checks, many of them worthless, from a friend of the family. The family had not complained to the police, but their evidence might help support a case brought by a military base that was not inclined to be so forgiving about receiving bad checks. The family was greatly impressed by the presence of an FBI agent, cooperative to the point of garrulousness, and eager with its offers of coffee and sandwiches (all of which the agent declined).

The most delicate interviews, however, are those in which an agent attempts to get a suspect to confess. In these cases, there are always two agents present to guard against later denials ("it's just his word against mine") or claims of mistreatment. Such interviews frequently arise in bank fraud cases. A bank officer or examiner finds a shortage and suspects a teller whose accounts are not in balance. The FBI is called. Two agents, after getting the background facts, will have a surprise interview at the bank with the teller. ("Surprise is an important factor," an agent explained. "It makes them nervous.") At this point the skill of the agents becomes important in whether the case is made (i.e., developed to the point that prosecution becomes possible). If the teller were steadfastly to deny everything, and if the loss were not so great as to warrant an elaborate investigation, it becomes difficult to make the case and the Bureau might well drop the matter. The suspect must first, of course, be advised of his or her rights, something the FBI has done since long before the Supreme Court, in the *Miranda* and other decisions, required this of all police departments.[11] One agent explained that at this point he likes to ask questions rapidly—"don't give them a chance to think up a story"—but without making promises or threats. Usually the evidence points strongly at the suspect; usually he or she confesses, sometimes with copious tears. Then it is vital to get the suspect to sign a statement so he or she cannot later repudiate the confession. If no confession is forthcoming, the agents may suggest a polygraph (i.e., "lie detector") test—"this often shakes them up." Of course, no person can be forced to submit to such a test, nor can his refusal be used as evidence against him, and in any event giving such a test requires high-level approval. But the psychological burden, to say nothing of the employment risk, of refusing to verify technologically one's innocence is often too great to bear, and either a test is held or a confession is forthcoming.

Despite their importance, interviewing skills are chiefly learned on the job. At one time, the FBI Academy gave to agent recruits little realistic instruction in interviewing. Only eight out of several hundred hours of training in the new agents' course at the FBI Academy were devoted to it. It was not until about 1975 that complaints from field agents and supervisors led the Academy to increase the hours of interview training to thirty and to make use of videotapes of each trainee's efforts. Even with this change, interview training consumes but 5 percent of the new agents' course and takes place entirely in an academic, rather than field, situation.

Whatever their skills, detectives are acutely aware that their task is not only tedious and time-consuming, but unlikely to produce any dramatic results. In one field office with about sixty agents doing general criminal investigative work, there were fewer than 220 convictions obtained during the course of the year, or a little more than three per agent, and two crimes—bank robbery and bank fraud—produced 40 percent of these. There were, of course, more FBI-initiated prosecutions than convictions and fewer prison sentences than convictions.

In most criminal matters, the FBI (or more accurately, the United States attorney acting on FBI information) wins

most of its cases. In the Federal District Court for Massachusetts in fiscal 1975, for example, all of the 18 bank em-
bezzlers, 10 of the 12 auto thieves, 16 of the 21 non-auto
thieves, and 10 of the 17 bank robbers were convicted; of the
68 persons prosecuted for these four major offenses, 79 percent were convicted. Of those convicted, however, fewer
than one half went to prison and fewer than one third were
sentenced to terms of three years or more.[12] And since, on
the average, a federal prisoner serves only one half of his
sentence, the actual time served was likely to be 18 months
or less for those imprisoned.[13] Like most detectives, FBI
agents express (privately) great dismay at the infrequency
and leniency of the sentences for those convicted of violating
federal law, especially since prosecutorial guidelines are
such that only the most serious cases are even taken to
court. But, again like most detectives, the agents do not
seem to let their dismay affect their performance: they are
told by their organization, and they believe themselves, that
their only job is to investigate. The *FBI Handbook* explicitly
states that agents "shall not urge prosecution," and various
United States attorneys confirm that FBI agents do not pressure them to prosecute. At the same time, the *Handbook*
also instructs agents to "discuss cases with the United States
attorney with sufficient aggressiveness to insure that the
Bureau's interests are protected."

Narcotics Agents as Instigators

The illegal sale of narcotics is a consensual act that ordinarily
produces no complainant and hence no indication to a law
enforcement agency that a crime has been committed. In
order to make an arrest, an investigator must first discover a

person who has committed, may be committing, or is intending to commit a crime and then arrange to observe (either firsthand or by means of an ally) its commission or discover a participant willing to admit his complicity. Sometimes the criminal act can be observed without having instigated its commission. There are two major observational methods that can lead to an arrest without first having to arrange for the crime to be committed: stakeouts and screening.[14]

A stakeout involves surreptitiously observing a criminal act being committed by persons unaware of the presence of law enforcement agents. If packets of heroin are sold on the street, for example, that can be observed and even photographed by agents. To do this requires advance knowledge that a crime will be committed in a certain place during a certain time period; such information can be gathered by informants or from intelligence. The difficulty with this strategy is that only low-level dealers traffic openly in a drug. Local police departments may make many arrests of such dealers, but federal narcotics agents believe their mission requires the arresting of higher-level dealers who rarely do business in public places or who do it only episodically, unpredictably, and after taking steps to ensure that they are not being observed. A clever dealer, for example, will take the money from the buyer in one location and then deliver the narcotic at another one, even by means of a third party, thereby making it difficult to establish, from observation alone, that a sale has taken place. At best the agents may be able only to charge the buyer with illegally possessing a drug, letting the dealer off scot-free. Furthermore, even if the complete transaction is observed, the arrested parties may be able to convince a judge that the evidence is insufficient to support a conviction. When the New York Police Department was making, in the 1960s, thousands of arrests of street-level heroin dealers, the vast majority were thrown out because of the claim that the evidence had been obtained by means of an illegal search by the arresting officer. They became known as "dropsie" cases, from the statement on the arrest report that the officer observed the suspect, when approached, to drop a packet of a substance later determined to be heroin.[15]

The other noninstigatory strategy is screening. Officers may discover illegal narcotics, perhaps even large amounts, as a result of a search. Making a traffic arrest, or apprehending a fugitive, may lead to the discovery of illegal drugs. This is a random and not a highly productive tactic, however, and the extent to which a person can be searched is sharply restricted by law. There is no general power to search on mere suspicion, and even a search incident to a valid arrest is limited as to its scope. To obtain a search warrant, one must first have reasonable grounds to believe that contraband will be found. Sometimes those grounds can be obtained from the tips of an informant or from other sources, but arrests made as a result of the execution of such a warrant will result in charging the suspect only with simple possession of a "controlled substance," and under federal law the maximum penalty for possession is but a year in prison and as a practical matter is much less.[16]

Screening is also performed by inspectors of the Customs Service and the Immigration Service. Since all heroin and many other controlled substances sold in the United States are imported into it, the baggage inspection and vessel search procedures of Customs officers can and do uncover large quantities of drugs. During 1975, 266 pounds of heroin, 744 pounds of cocaine, and nearly 700,000 pounds of marijuana were removed at ports and borders by Customs and Immigration officers.[17] Customs officers have two advantages over other law enforcement investigators in operating a screening strategy: they work at points (ports and borders) where the flow of contraband is somewhat more spatially concentrated, and they enjoy the right to search persons and property without a warrant and without making an arrest. (The degree to which contraband such as drugs is concentrated at border crossings is only marginally greater than on city streets, and thus the Customs advantage in this respect is only relative. Drugs constitute but a tiny fraction of all the goods flowing through ports and air terminals; no random-search procedure, and even no such procedure aided by shrewd judgment and drug-sniffing dogs, is likely to uncover more than a small fraction of the illicit merchandise.)

Useful as this screening strategy is, it has its limits. Being dependent on luck, instinct, or tips, it cannot reach more than a small fraction of the illegal drugs crossing a border. Because no illegal sale is observed, the offenders can only be charged with simple possession. And most important, the persons carrying the contraband are likely to be umimportant couriers—"mules"—whose arrest has little impact on the operation of the importing and distributing organization.

Because of the limitations of stakeout and screening strategies and because federal narcotics investigators are members of an agency—the Drug Enforcement Administration—that has the mission of bringing to justice "those *organizations,* and principal members of *organizations* involved in the growing, manufacture or distribution of controlled substances appearing in or destined for the illicit traffic in the United States,"[18] the dominant strategy of these investigators is not that of detecting or randomly observing a crime but of instigating one under controlled circumstances.

A narcotics case typically begins with a tip, sometimes from an ordinary citizen but usually from an informant, that drugs are being illegally manufactured, bought, or sold. The agent who develops the tip has the case, unless his group supervisor for some reason decides to assign it to someone else. The agent begins by getting as much information as possible from the informant and then attempting to make an undercover buy. In areas where drugs are sold in high volume to many customers with relative impunity, the agent may approach the dealer uninvited and try to "score" (make a buy). Usually, however, dealers are suspicious of strangers, even ones dressed and acting in the style of a street person. The agent will then induce the informant to introduce him to the dealer—"to duke him in"—and perhaps even help arrange the buy. The agent working undercover is always accompanied by a partner who will corroborate the transaction and protect the other agent. The money used for this buy is drawn from agency funds ("PE/PI" money—Purchase of Evidence/Purchase of Information), the serial numbers of which are recorded.

The initial buy is often for a small amount of the drug and is rarely followed by an arrest. The agent prefers to defer an arrest until he can seize a large amount of drugs or can implicate higher-ups in the distributional system or both. Furthermore, if the agent can show that a person has sold illegal drugs on two or more occasions, it strengthens the prosecutor's case and makes more likely a conviction for trafficking, for which the maximum penalty may be fifteen years in prison, instead of simple possession.[19] Finally, the agent has some interest in protecting his informant, and this is more easily done if the arrest—"the bust"—occurs some time after the agent has first been duked in. (If the agent is especially concerned about the informant, he can arrange a "double duke"—after he has made an undercover buy, he can then duke in a second undercover agent for the second or subsequent buys.)

Ideally, the agent wants to work his way up the distribution system, by pretending to want larger supplies so he can go into business himself, until he can implicate with eyewitness testimony all of the members of a drug-trafficking organization. Rarely is the ideal realized. Some dealers will not reveal their sources for fear of acquiring, in the person of the undercover agent, a competitor. Other dealers are willing to run the risk of dealing with an agent but unwilling to risk introducing a possible agent to their suppliers—the penalties exacted by the supplier are likely to be greater, and certainly swifter, than what might be imposed by a prosecutor. Moreover, higher-ranking dealers are often more wary than street dealers. The latter are often drug users or addicts themselves and deal in order to get supplies for their own use. Wholesalers are rarely addicts, have more to lose, and often will not accept the introduction of a new "dealer" to them. Many of the most important dealers never handle drugs personally, and therefore it would be impossible to incriminate them by arranging an illegal transaction.

There are ways of making cases against narcotics organizations other than through working one's way up the chain of distribution by making undercover purchases. One is to arrest a violator who is knowledgeable about the entire apparatus and who can be induced to testify against his colleagues. Ordinarily, the only inducement available is plea bargaining—a promise of leniency in exchange for incriminating testimony. Recruiting a defendant-witness is similar to recruiting an informant; both will be discussed in chapter 3. It is important to note, however, that building a case in this way requires corroborating evidence and that the proportion of arrestees able and willing to testify against key members of an organization is small. Interestingly, it is often easier to build cases this way against marijuana and dangerous-drug (barbiturate and amphetamine) dealers than against heroin organizations because the former are more likely to be small, relatively self-contained enterprises involving persons almost all of whom are American citizens and thus more easily arrested.

Another method is to build a conspiracy case against identified traffickers. Under federal law, a person "who attempts or conspires to commit" an offense involving the illegal manufacture, distribution, or dispensing of a drug can be punished as if he had actually done so.[20] To prove a conspiracy, an agent must establish that a group acted in concert and that at least one overt act was committed in furtherance of the conspiracy. The testimony of one of the conspirators can be used to help establish the fact of a conspiracy; so also can showing patterns of communication and movement among the group that are consistent with the ends of the conspiracy. This evidence might be derived from a close scrutiny of long-distance telephone toll slips, airplane and hotel reservation records, and photographs of meetings. But the most compelling evidence of a conspiracy are the words of the conspirators themselves, acquired by means of electronic surveillance.

A wiretap (intercepting a telephone call) or a "bug" (recording the conversation in a room) can be obtained legally only with a court order issued by a judge after an application by the agent has been approved by the United States attorney general.[21] The application must show that the agents have probable cause to believe that the conversations to be intercepted will bear on the commission of an offense; usually, an informant's statement is the basis of this showing. Once granted—and a reasonable application is rarely denied—the operation of a tap or bug is a costly and time-consuming process. Ten or more agents—one or two entire enforcement groups—will be occupied by the tasks attendant to managing a wire. Two agents will listen and operate the recording equipment, two more will watch the premises in order to identify who is entering and leaving and who may be using the telephone, and two more will be available to follow persons leaving the premises in order to establish their behavior subsequent to the overheard conversation. Four to six additional agents must be available to provide relief for the first shift. Owing to the cost of a wire, they are relatively rare—during 1975, the DEA as a whole had fewer than three dozen in operation around the country. They are more likely to be used in cases involving the movement of drugs over substantial distances and therefore requiring the services of a dispersed criminal organization that necessarily arranges its affairs by telephone.

The limitations of stakeout and screening methods, the

difficulty of finding a defendant able to testify against an entire organization, the laboriousness of building conspiracy cases, and the cost of a wiretap mean that to the extent a narcotics agent desires to make arrests, they will be "buy-and-bust" cases. As we shall see, for a variety of reasons not well understood in the agency but to which all agency members are keenly sensitive, there is a felt pressure to produce arrests and drug seizures. As a result, agents will make two or three undercover buys from a dealer and then arrest him in the act, seizing the drugs and recovering some of the buy money.

The DEA assigns arrested drug violators to one of four classifications according to their importance in the traffic. A Class I violator is the head of an illicit laboratory or smuggling organization or a dealer in large quantities of high-purity drugs. Class II includes the larger illicit drug wholesalers. Class III is made up of distributors at the sub-wholesale level—typically, persons dealing in ounce bags of heroin or the equivalent of other drugs. Class IV is a residual category for violators who do not meet the criteria for a higher class. During the last half of 1975, the DEA acting alone made 1,518 domestic heroin arrests; of these, 77 percent were of Class III or Class IV violators. The typical arrest—65 percent of the total—was of a Class III violator.

The apparent emphasis on "buy-and-bust" cases is a constant source of controversy and policymaking in the DEA. What is striking is that everybody—agents, supervisors, regional directors, and headquarters executives—agrees that the organization should be making cases against high-level violators and criminal organizations. Despite this agreement, and despite considerable pressure from Congress and other external sources to make big cases, the statistics seem to suggest an emphasis on small cases. As a result, DEA members spend a not inconsiderable amount of time blaming each other or outside influences for the large number of Class III violators apprehended. In chapter 4, the reasons for this problem will be discussed.

The day-to-day task of the narcotics agent is not dominated by these policy questions, however, but by the routines he must employ to initiate *any* case, high or low. No
matter what technique—wiretaps, conspiracy prosecutions,
plea bargaining—is ultimately employed and no matter how
significant the traffickers finally arrested, most drug cases,
except for lucky breaks, must begin with inducing some
street-level violator to make an illegal drug sale. And that, in
turn, begins with an informant.

Sometimes the informant—technically, the "cooperating
individual," or CI—is a law-abiding person who has useful
information, as when the legal manufacturer of a chemical
used in the production of amphetamines or barbiturates
notes a suspicious purchase of large quantities of the precur-
sor and alerts agents to the possible existence of a clandestine laboratory. But ordinarily, the informant is himself illegally involved in drug trafficking, supplying a lead out of a
variety of motives (see chapter 3). Usually the informant cooperates knowingly, but sometimes he is an unwitting informant—a street dealer who is unaware that he is dealing
with an agent and who unintentionally introduces him to a
supplier.

The critical skill of a narcotics agent is the ability to persuade a person involved in crime to supply information that
is not ordinarily to his advantage to reveal or to engage in a
transaction that is not in his interest to consummate. The
skills required to acquire the information or complete the
transactions are related but somewhat different. For the former, the agent must be dependable, making and keeping
promises, and supportive; for the latter, he must be devious,
dissembling, and artful. The witting informant must be able
to trust his agent, the unwitting dealer must *believe* he can
trust him. To the former the agent must make credible his
ability to influence the threats and opportunities that collaboration with the law entail, while to the latter he must make
convincing his portrayal of a street hustler knowledgeable in
the idiom and manner of traffickers. To achieve this last goal,

the agent must appear and dress in the style of the street: narcotics agents, unlike FBI agents, will dress flamboyantly, have long hair, beards, and mustaches, and speak the language of the underworld. On a case, women become "chicks" or "broads" and traffickers "dudes"; an unreliable or small-scale dealer is a "creep," a serious dealer is a "righteous crook." The informant is (though never to his face) a "snitch" or a "twist." When the illegal transaction occurs, the case has "gone down"; a person when arrested is "taken off."

The exercise of these skills routinely exposes the agent to risks: certainly of exposure, perhaps of injury, possibly of death. Since 1930, when the Federal Bureau of Narcotics was founded, seventeen agents have been killed in the line of duty, almost as many as in the FBI even though the latter has had a longer history and at least four times as many agent personnel. A narcotics agent, like a big-city patrolman, is always on his guard, suspicious and wary. His authority does not depend, as with the FBI agent, on his office or, as with the patrolman, on his uniform, but rather on his demeanor: he must personally take control of situations by his manner and bearing. (In this, he is not utterly unlike the patrolman; the latter's uniform does not in all places confer authority adequate to his task.)

Offsetting these difficulties is the excitement of the hunt. Far more than with investigators or patrolmen, instigators enact at periodic intervals a complex drama involving tempting the quarry, setting the hook, playing the line, and finally netting the captive. The proceedings are the legal analogue of a confidence game, with one difference: the con man abandons the "mark," while the instigator attempts to convert him. Two typical chases in which I participated are illustrative. In one, an agent and his informant agreed to buy a large amount of cocaine. The meeting was set for a restaurant. Beforehand, other agents in cars staked out the area. While in the dining room, however, the informant received a phone call changing the meeting place to a public park nearby. The "buyers" set out for the park, but now the covering agents had to improvise a new plan for surveillance and capture and do so without benefit of direct conversation with the buying agent, since approaching him directly might alert any member of the drug gang who might be observing. The "buyers" stopped in the park area, and there ensued a lengthy wait; two agents played Frisbee on the grass, others slumped in nearby cars. Nothing happened. Finally the informant spotted his dealer, but the latter left without stopping. The agents, though they would have preferred to catch him in the act of selling, decided that arresting him with the cocaine in his possession was better than nothing, especially since a large amount was supposedly involved. They gave chase, but the dealer eluded them—he knew the park, they did not, and by running he managed to reach a hidden car the agents could not identify and hence could not pursue. Box score: ten agents tied up for an entire day, nothing to show for it.

The second case involved more elaborate preparations by both agents and traffickers. A Boston agent was duked into a dealer of large quantities of LSD. The dealer agreed to make a delivery, but only in San Francisco. Suspecting that the clandestine laboratory might be located there, the DEA dispatched the Boston agents to the West Coast where they joined local agents. A hotel room was rented in which to make the buy, but when the dealer appeared he insisted the undercover agents accompany him to another location. Had the agents been making a routine contact with a dealer, they might have worn a "wire" (i.e., concealed transmitter) so as to guide their colleagues, but being so close to a score they did not want to risk ruining what looked like a big buy in case the dealer should search them. The covering agents thus had to follow the dealer's car with the undercover agents inside, but this time through the streets of San Francisco. A DEA airplane hovered overhead carrying a vio-

lently airsick agent who radioed directions to the surveillance cars. The cars had to take turns "driving point"
(i.e., being in close visual contact with the driver's car) so as
not to reveal the pursuit. The dealer stopped at a house. The
agents had to decide whether the buy was going down there,
in which case they should close in for the arrest, or whether
the dealer was stopping to get a drink, change cars, or meet
a friend, in which case closing in would ruin the entire
operation. Nervously, the agents decided to wait. Soon, the
dealer and the undercover officers emerged, entered another car, and drove off. The pursuit resumed. Finally, the
dealer stopped near a parked van and got out, accompanied
by the "buyers," who gave a prearranged hand signal. The
deal was going down. The agents rushed in and arrested the
dealer and the occupants of the van. It was a noisy, confus-
ing scene, and nothing indicated that the long-haired men in
mod clothes brandishing guns were law officers. A passerby
demanded to know what was happening; a crowd began to
gather, curious and to a degree unfriendly. The agents
gruffly ordered them on their way, and the bystanders,
who by now could see the badges the agents had hurriedly
clipped to their shirt pockets, obeyed.

For most agents, these are the moments of satisfaction.
On a big case, two or more groups of agents, sometimes an
entire office, will be involved. But the key roles are played
by the men working undercover, and not all or even most
agents are skilled at this. In a DEA office, a few agents will
have many informants, will frequently work undercover,
and will set up many buys, while others will go through the
motions until a case is going down, when they will be en-
listed to play back-up roles in the chase. In one DEA office,
for example, eleven agents, comprising one third of the non-
supervisory enforcement personnel, had during 1973–74 recruited 71 percent of the informants. Four agents (12 percent of the total) accounted for 37 percent of the informants.
Informant development is, for DEA agents, a skill as impor-

tant as interviewing methods for FBI agents, yet there is little evidence that either organization attempts systematically to discover why some have the skill or to develop that skill in others.

Nor has the DEA devoted much effort to training agents in the art of developing informants. In 1974, only seven hours in the basic agent class out of a total of more than five hundred were devoted explicitly to informants and only three to interrogation. (There were, in addition, some practical exercises that touched, to an unknown degree, on informant relations.) In the DEA as in the FBI, basic training emphasizes rules, laws, firearms, and physical skills.

DEA agents are charged with enforcing laws governing the production and distribution of scores of drugs, categorized by statute into various "schedules" related to their presumed degree of dangerousness.[22] The DEA for management purposes groups these substances into four categories: heroin, cocaine, marijuana/hashish, and "dangerous drugs" (amphetamines, barbiturates, and dozens of other controlled substances). The agents, however, think of themselves as being, as many put it, part of the "Bureau of Heroin"; that drug is the preferred target, an arrest of a major heroin dealer confers great status among peers, and in the competition for scarce resources (such as "buy" money) having a big heroin case is thought to give one an advantage. This view is reinforced by periodic statements from public officials about the seriousness of the heroin problem.

This emphasis is not readily apparent from DEA statistics, in large part because for many years the DEA included among its arrests cases begun by other agencies (the Customs Service or the Immigration and Naturalization Service) but referred to the DEA for completion. Of the 7,500 arrests made by the DEA in the second half of 1975, about half (3,700) were made by the DEA acting alone on cases it initiated; of these, 41 percent were of heroin violators and only 17 percent were of marijuana/hashish violators. By contrast, of the 1,268 arrests made in cases referred to the DEA from Customs or the INS, only 9 percent were of heroin violators and 73 percent were of marijuana/hashish violators. The reason for the disparity is clear: heroin and marijuana of equivalent financial value differ greatly in bulk so that a major trafficking organization seeking to import a profitable amount of the latter finds it more difficult to conceal it from detection by Customs/INS screening procedures.

The incentive system and peer-group attitudes among DEA agents today support the emphasis on heroin as they supported it a dozen years earlier when the agency was much smaller and called the Federal Bureau of Narcotics. This has meant that efforts of DEA administrators to direct more attention to dangerous drugs have not met with great success. "Pill cases" are thought by many agents to involve only "kiddie dope," even though the medical dangers posed by, for example, barbiturate addiction are often quite serious. Few agents would pass up an opportunity to take off a major dealer in LSD or "speed" or to close down a large clandestine laboratory. But few agents would pass up a chance to arrest a major heroin dealer in order to get the pill supplier. Only 16 percent of the arrests made by the DEA alone during the last half of 1975 were of dangerous-drug violators.

In apparent contradiction to the heroin emphasis in the DEA has been the steady increase in the arrests made of cocaine dealers. Between 1972 and 1975, cocaine arrests (by the DEA alone) increased by over 47 percent while heroin arrests remained about constant. As a result, whereas cocaine arrests were only half as numerous as heroin arrests in 1972, they were about equally frequent in 1974.[23] There are several possible explanations—that the DEA or its agents decided to "go after" cocaine, that heroin was temporarily in short supply owing to the cutback in the Turkish opium crop, that cocaine became more common on the street and arrests rose automatically as a consequence of following tra-

ditional but changeable operating procedures, or that cocaine became more available and arrests increased because
of operating procedures that could not feasibly have been
modified to produce any other result. An answer to this
question must be postponed until the other organizational
and strategic elements of the DEA are discussed.

DEA agents, like FBI agents, work under guidelines established, formally or informally, by local prosecutors. In
one large city, for example, the United States attorney will
not accept for federal prosecution a DEA case involving less
than an ounce of seized heroin or cocaine or less than ten
pounds of marijuana or five pounds of hashish. As with FBI
cases, DEA arrests involve shared jurisdiction. Since drug
dealing is also illegal under state law, local authorities could
in principle prosecute in local courts those cases declined by
federal prosecutors. In fact it is uncommon for a DEA agent
to turn over to a city detective a case too small for federal
prosecution. The agent will either not make an arrest in the
first place because the amounts are so small or else he will
keep the case alive in the hope that eventually the arrestee
will lead the agent to larger dealers who can then be arrested for handling amounts that are within the prosecutor's
guidelines. This means that, depending on the vigor of local
police narcotics squads, a large number of small dealers may
operate freely in a city with even a large cadre of federal narcotics agents.

There is a difference in the impact of prosecutive guidelines on DEA and FBI agents, however. An FBI case for
which prosecution is declined means less work for the
agent—he knows before he makes much of an investigation
at all whether it will merit prosecution. The closed case has,
typically, no further significance. The decision to prosecute
or not exhausts the FBI agent's bureaucratic interest in the
matter, whatever his personal feelings about the blamewor-
thiness of the crime. But knowing the prosecutive guidelines
in advance does not always help the narcotics agent conserve

his efforts, for often only by expending those efforts—sometimes over a long period—can he discover whether an informant or an arrestee will be able to "give up" an ounce dealer, a kilo dealer, a major importer, or nobody but the addict who lives next door. By the time a prosecutor declines to take the case, the agent has often invested many hours of work, perhaps many dollars of buy money, and certainly much emotional commitment. Furthermore, narcotics cases are linked one to another because of the possibility that any given case may be an entry into a large network of cases. Thus, for DEA agents there is rarely any such thing as a "closed" case—the agent keeps many cases active, at least in his mind, in the hope of developing an informant or a lead into a bigger case. If the original case is not prosecuted, one important incentive he can use to produce that informant—the threat of jail—is foreclosed.

These differences in task explain why FBI agents can accept prosecutorial decisions with greater equanimity (if not with greater approval) than DEA agents.

To their dismay over prosecutive guidelines DEA agents add their disgust over judicial sentencing. Whether they are entitled to these feelings depends, of course, on how serious one believes narcotics offenses to be. The table opposite shows the dispositions in all federal courts during 1975 of the three major kinds of drug cases and, for comparison, four major federal criminal cases in which the FBI typically conducts the investigation. (Not all drug cases shown are the result of DEA investigations, however; some may arise from Customs or the INS. In the great majority, however, the DEA either initiated or completed the case.)

About 80 to 90 percent of FBI-initiated prosecutions result in convictions; the figure is slightly lower for drug cases—75 to 79 percent. Whether this is because of judicial leniency or the greater opportunities available for defense in a drug case is not clear. A drug defendant usually has more opportunities to raise procedural motions than a bank robber

Disposition of Defendants on Selected Charges
in United States District Courts, 1975

CHARGES	DEFEN-DANTS NO.	CONVICTED NO.	CONVICTED %	PRISON NO.	PRISON %	3 YEARS+ NO.	3 YEARS+ %
General Offenses							
Auto theft	1861	1530	82	1041	68	690	66
Bank embezzlement	1117	1010	90	174	17	57	33
Bank robbery	2234	1853	83	1668	90	1585	95
Theft from interstate shipments	1254	990	79	357	36	178	50
Drug Abuse Prevention and Control Act							
Marijuana	3741	2830	76	1529	54	576	38
Narcotics	5217	3925	75	2626	67	1788	68
Controlled substances	1666	1318	79	683	52	407	60

Source: *1975 Annual Report of the Director*, Administrative Office of the United States Courts, Washington, D.C., tables D4, D5.

or an auto thief—it is easier to allege entrapment, illegal searches and seizures, and unauthorized wiretaps when the case is made by an instigator rather than an investigator. Furthermore, drug cases often involve groups of defendants, some of whom may be able to persuade a judge that they were not materially involved in the trafficking.

Only half of those convicted in federal court of trafficking illegally in marijuana or dangerous drugs are imprisoned; two thirds of those convicted on narcotics charges (usually, heroin or cocaine) are imprisoned. Given the guidelines that require, in many jurisdictions, large amounts of a drug to be involved before prosecution is even commenced, DEA agents are understandably disheartened when a third to a half of those convicted "get a walk." Of those imprisoned, only a third of the marijuana dealers but up to two thirds of the narcotics and "pill" dealers are sentenced to three years or more. (Actual time served will, of course, be much less— about half of the sentence on the average.) The combined probability of facing a prison sentence of three years or more if convicted ranges from one chance in five on marijuana charges to nearly one chance in two on narcotics charges. By these measures, the federal courts appear to regard narcotics trafficking about as seriously as interstate shipment of stolen motor vehicles and much less seriously than bank robbery (where a convicted person will almost certainly get a three-year or longer prison sentence).

The results vary among federal district courts. In Massachusetts, for example, the probability of going to prison if convicted on a narcotics charge is less than one in two (.44) compared to three chances in four (.75) nationally, and the chances of getting a sentence of three years or more if convicted is only one in seven (.14) compared to nearly one chance in two (.46) nationally. Boston DEA agents, accordingly, view Massachusetts federal judges as hopelessly "soft"; federal prosecutors in Boston, on the other hand, regard local DEA agents as preoccupied with "trivial" cases (Class III and Class IV violators). One assistant United States attorney described the Boston DEA office as "just interested in statistics" that it produces by "little buy-and-bust cases." Agents counter by complaining that a person dealing even in ounces of heroin is hardly a small fry (the street value of an ounce of pure heroin is about $47,000 after it has been cut and distributed).

The Tasks of Investigators: A Summary

Though both FBI and DEA agents "enforce laws" and "apprehend offenders," the actual behavior and critical tasks of the agents, and thus the administrative and executive problems posed for the respective agencies, are quite different.

FBI agents assigned to general criminal matters are detectives who screen reports generated by other organizations (and, occasionally, by individual victims) and select, by applying organizationally defined criteria, events that warrant nontrivial responses. DEA agents rarely receive complaints from organizations or individuals that credibly allege a serious law infraction; instead, the narcotics agents must create their own workload by inducing individuals to reveal information they would prefer to keep confidential or to engage in transactions they, if fully informed and free to behave autonomously, would avoid.

Detectives, such as FBI agents, know with reasonable confidence that a crime has been committed; their task is to find who is responsible and to produce credible evidence of his culpability. Instigators, such as DEA agents, know with reasonable confidence that one or more persons has committed or is about to commit a crime; their task is to observe its commission, usually by creating, under controlled conditions, a suitable opportunity. Detectives gather information by interviewing persons, most of whom are innocent citizens. Obtaining that information from such persons is made easier if the agents appear trustworthy and conventional. Instigators deal primarily with persons who probably have broken or are about to break laws, often as part of an ongoing enterprise. Obtaining the cooperation of these persons requires the investigator to appear clever, "hip," or threatening.

A crucial issue is whether the tasks of FBI and DEA agents *need* be as different as they are. Many critics of narcotics enforcement believe that important cases can be made by investigative rather than instigative methods; as we shall see in chapters 4 and 5, that has even been an issue among DEA administrators. Strictly speaking, drug trafficking could be investigated by the same methods as cases involving stolen securities or illegal gambling—develop an informant, install wiretaps, trace the movements of conspirators, seize physical evidence, put criminals under surveillance. It is my impression, from brief research trips abroad, that narcotics officers in England and France may function in just this way and thus quite differently than their American counterparts. But what is logically possible is not, within the American context, always feasible. The essential problem is that whereas other nations have either a national police force (as does France) or at least a single police force for each city (as in England), police responsibilities in the United States are divided among local, state, and federal authorities, each with a constitutionally distinct basis for existence. Federalism, in short, creates a system of different and even rival police organizations sharing powers over common problems.

Most investigations depend on informants; narcotics investigations depend crucially on them. Where a jurisdiction has a single police force, that organization can both develop and use informants for its inquiries. The leads for narcotics cases could come, not from undercover buys, but from other police activities. In a federal system, a national police agency such as the DEA or FBI must either obtain informants from state and local agencies or develop its own. Borrowing informants from another, and rival, police agency is difficult and often impossible; it would be as if the Ford Motor Company expected to borrow its auto designers from General Motors. Therefore, in the United States, federal police agencies for the most part must produce their own informants. How this is done will be explained in the next chapter. For now, what is important is that DEA agents see no practical way of finding informants other than by arresting street-level dealers after making undercover drug buys. This belief leads DEA agents to define their central task as one of making buys. And as we shall see, powerful peer-group pressures and organizational traditions tend to reinforce that definition and render it exceptionally resistant to change.

The execution of both FBI and DEA tasks necessarily involves a good deal of discretion: a detective can choose, within limits, what kinds of cases to make the object of his most extensive interviewing efforts; an instigator can choose, within limits, how hard to press an informant to give up another dealer, what buys are worth making, and when the time is ripe for an arrest.

Both detectives and instigators are exposed to opportunities for corruption, but the latter far more than the former. The detective, were he to accept money or favors to act other than as his duty required, would have to conceal or alter information about a crime already known to his organization. The instigator can easily agree to overlook offenses known to him but to no one else or to participate in illegal transactions (buying and selling drugs) for his own rather than for the organization's advantage.

The problem for the administrators of investigative agencies is to control the behavior of operators—the agents. This involves obtaining valid information about what the agents do, comparing that information to some reasonable standard, and issuing instructions that alter behavior, where necessary, in the direction of the standard. Obviously, the administrative control of police patrolmen would be—and in fact is—quite difficult: the order-maintenance and service-delivery functions of the patrolman are carried on out of sight of the organization and produce few measures (such as "crimes known" or "arrests") of what in fact happens. But for investigators, the problems ought to be much less. FBI agents, at least in their criminal work, respond only to crimes that can be either solved or not solved, and when solved there is likely to be an arrest and possibly a conviction. DEA agents make cases that vary, in measurable ways, in their value and significance, and one case can lead, again in observable ways, to one or more additional cases of measurable importance.

In chapter 4, we shall see to what extent these agencies are in fact administered by measuring results; if they are, to what effect, and if they are not, for what reasons. The answer to these questions has more than merely intellectual significance, for on the ability and willingness of administrators to control effectively the behavior of subordinates, especially subordinates exercising the formidable powers of detectives, depends the public's confidence that its goals are served.

CHAPTER

3

Informants

HAVING productive informants is essential in many FBI cases, indispensable in virtually all DEA cases. Differences in the ability to develop and utilize this vital resource accounts, more than any other factor, for differences in the success of investigators. FBI cases are sometimes solved because the victim can identify a suspect or because the criminal exposes himself by trying to sell his loot to a suspicious buyer, but where there is no victim identification (i.e., the case is "unsub") and no incriminating sale of booty, the agent having the case is usually helpless unless he can find a knowledgeable informant. Where such an informant can be found, the results are sometimes spectacular, as when the FBI solved the 1972 robbery of the Hotel Pierre in New York City in which at least $4 million in cash and jewels were taken. The daring theft, masterfully planned and executed, became something less than a complete success when the robbers took the jewels to a fence who turned out to be a high-level FBI informant.[1] And sometimes the informant system can backfire, as when various persons surface to claim, with some plausibility, that they had been informants in various political movements, some of which, though ideologically extreme, were hardly criminal or seditious conspiracies.[2]

Strictly speaking, "informant" is too broad a label to fit the various kinds of persons who provide information. The FBI distinguishes among "confidential sources" (noncriminal persons in legitimate occupations who provide information without any special inducement) and "informants" (persons with close contacts to criminals or other investigative targets and with a proven ability to supply information). An agent, with the approval of his supervisor, may open a file designating a person an informant after that person has already given some valuable information. An informant knows of his or her relationship with the FBI and is subject to certain rules, such as paying income taxes on money received from the Bureau.[3] Until recently, the FBI also had a category for "potential criminal informants" (PCIs) made up of persons identified by agents, perhaps without the persons knowing it, as possible future sources of information. Relatively few PCIs were ever promoted to the status of informants; for a long time, the category had meaning chiefly as a "statistical accomplishment" to which agents had to contribute.

The DEA distinguishes between Class I informants, who have themselves a criminal background or criminal connections, and Class II informants, who are ordinary citizens who may have observed something of significance. The vast majority of informants carried on the register of a local DEA office are in Class I.

Criminal informants serve three functions. One is simply as a source of leads as to the behavior of a suspect, the identity of a violator, or the location of the loot. A second is to deceive other criminals by introducing them to undercover agents pretending to be criminals or by stimulating would-be offenders to commit a crime while being observed by agents. These are sometimes called "participating informants." A third is to testify in court against criminal accomplices; these are referred to as "informant defendants." The FBI and the DEA both use informants for the first and third purposes, but only the DEA uses them extensively for the second.

The law governing police use of informants is complex, as would be expected when society seeks to balance two competing objectives—in this case, guaranteeing a fair trial to persons accused as a result of evidence gathered with the aid of informants and ensuring that law enforcement can be effective. The conflict arises when a defendant seeks to have an informant identified in court and the police seek to maintain the informant's anonymity.

The Supreme Court has consistently supported the right of the police to employ informants and to use them to gather information from unwitting suspects. The Fourth Amendment does not protect "a wrongdoer's misplaced belief that a person to whom he voluntarily confides his wrongdoing will not reveal it."[4] This use of an informant is constitutional, even if he records what the suspect says to him on a concealed recording device.[5] Finally, the Court has upheld in general the right of the police to maintain the anonymity of persons who furnish information to the authorities.[6]

But there are limits to the protection afforded the informant. In the *Rovario* case, decided in 1957, the Court held that an informant's information is not privileged—i.e., entitled to confidentiality—"where the disclosure of an informer's identity, or of the contents of his communication, is relevant and helpful to the defense of an accused, or is essential to a fair determination of a case."[7]

This last proviso seemed to open the door for the wholesale disclosure of informant identities, even though the Court was careful to state that its holding in *Rovario* was not a fixed rule but a criterion that had to be balanced, on a case-by-case basis, with other criteria, including the public interest in protecting the flow of vital information to the police. Such a balancing test is, of course, an invitation to controversy and appeals. Ten years later, the Court set some clearer limits to how far the balance could swing. In *McCray* v. *Illinois*,[8] it decided that when the police apply to a judge for an arrest or search warrant, they can establish that they have probable cause to believe the suspect guilty or the

dwelling to hide some contraband if they have credible information from a reliable informant. Even if this is the only
source of evidence of probable cause, the police need not
reveal the informant's identity.

It is much less clear what circumstances entitle the police
to conceal an informant's identity *at the trial.* The defense
has no absolute right to secure the appearance of the informant; should he appear and give evidence, however, he
must identify himself and be subject to cross-examination.[9]
Between these extremes, a number of lower-court rulings
has begun to produce a consensus that, though not yet reviewed by the Supreme Court, is probably a reliable indication of the prevailing rule of law. Much depends on the purposes for which the informant was used. If he was merely
the source of a tip about a crime or its possible perpetrator,
he may expect to remain anonymous.[10] If, on the other
hand, the informant was an eyewitness to or otherwise an
immediate participant in the illegal transaction, then there is
a strong presumption that he will have to be identified.[11] In
between, different circumstances make for different rules.
If, for example, the informant introduced the undercover
agent to the trafficker and then departed before the transaction was made, the privilege of the informant to remain
anonymous will depend on how important his testimony
may be to clearly establishing the identity, or in other ways
showing the guilt or innocence, of the dealer.[12]

In short, investigators, such as FBI agents, who use an informant to identify a suspect or obtain a warrant, can use
their informants confidentially, but instigators, such as DEA
agents, who typically induce a drug trafficker to make an
illegal sale, must often, if an informant assisted in that transaction, reveal the informant's identity. This distinction
creates a special problem for DEA agents and contributes to
an important difference in the way in which FBI and DEA
agents manage their tasks.

Overwhelmingly, informants are recruited from among

persons who are themselves criminals or closely connected with criminals. Though occasionally the FBI will find a confidential source who is helpful (e.g., a bartender who can help agents keep track of suspicious persons who frequent his establishment) and the DEA will find a Class II informant who provides good leads (e.g., a hotel manager who advises agents whenever a suspected trafficker is in town), the informants who make cases by identifying hitherto unknown perpetrators or supplying important evidence or leads are those who themselves have guilty knowledge. Indeed, FBI and DEA agents alike often complain (never publicly) about public-spirited citizens, many of whom are "police buffs," who fancy themselves sleuths and who call frequently to recount useless information and baseless suspicions. A citizen with a bona fide lead on a criminal investigation is always welcome, and many cases have been solved with his help, but the self-appointed "informant" is usually greeted with weary dismay.

A major motive—most investigators believe *the* major motive—of an informant is to obtain leniency on a criminal charge in exchange for information about accomplices involved in that charge or persons involved in other criminal offenses. I reviewed the records in one local office of the DEA of all the informants, thirty-nine in number, who had been recruited in the years 1970–72 and who were still active in 1974. They were typical, not of all informants, but of the most productive and long-lasting ones. Twenty of the thirty-nine were "working off a beef"—cooperating in exchange for having charges dropped or lessened, or milder sentences imposed, on criminal matters they faced. Not all of these "beefs" were drug related and not all of the twenty had been recruited by the DEA itself—two had been arrested by the FBI on other criminal charges, one by the Secret Service for counterfeiting, two by Immigration and Naturalization for being illegal aliens, and two by other law enforcement agencies. Thirteen of the twenty, however, were working off a drug charge. Those not facing charges had a variety of motives: nine simply were seeking money (one even described himself proudly as a "professional informer"), two claimed ideological motives (they were anti-Castro activists), one was seeking help in getting American citizenship, and the remainder, five, were police buffs or public-spirited citizens who liked the idea of helping agents catch drug dealers.

Most narcotics agents believe that an informant working off a beef is the only productive one; the threat of going to jail is, in their eyes, a greater inducement than the promise of small sums of money. An informant so motivated is a "twist." Even so, informants facing charges are paid for their information, if it is useful, just as are persons not facing charges, partly because the money increases the motivation to cooperate and partly because many of those working as informants are low-level dealers who genuinely need the money in order to make ends meet. Setting aside two informants who made some very large cases and were paid handsomely, the total amount paid to the average twist and money-seeker taken together was, at the time of the survey, about $1,000, with many receiving no more than $100 or $200.

An experienced narcotics agent who had responsibility for overseeing the informant program in one local office was convinced that twists were, in general, the only good informants, and not even all of these were. "The civic-minded guys are useless—being law-abiding, they don't know anything about the drug traffic. And the money-seekers are unreliable because you have no real hold over them. They may try to set you up just for the money, and if they do, you have no way of getting back at them." The data from this office would seem to bear him out: *all* of the twenty twists but only ten of the nineteen "volunteers" in my sample had made cases (that is, provided useful evidence against other, and often bigger, dealers).

Though most of the long-term informants and most of the productive informants seem to be twists, the majority of informants are not, nor do most arrests produce informants. During 1972, another local DEA office arrested 234 persons on drug charges, only eleven of whom became informants. However, during that year a total of seventy-two informants were recruited—eleven from among those arrested, seventeen from other law enforcement agencies (including other DEA offices), and forty-three from various kinds of volunteers (money-seekers, relatives of addicts wanting revenge against the dealer, drug dealers hoping to put rivals out of business, and public-spirited citizens). Seventeen of these informants never produced any cases, and within two years a total of sixty-four had become inactive. Of the eight who remained active, only two were still working off beefs; the remainder were working for money.

The contrast between the two DEA offices in the motives of long-term, productive informants can be explained in part by the skills and inclinations of the recruiting agents. A single agent in the second office had recruited three of the eight long-term informants and over a three-year period had recruited a total of thirteen informants, more than any other street agent in the office. Moreover, he had recruited most of the useful black informants (the agent was himself black) and many of those who had made the biggest heroin cases. To this agent, pay and "sweet talk" were more useful incentives than a beef. Facing charges might provide the leverage to first recruit the informant, but if he is to be useful over the long haul other incentives must be used. In this, managing informants is little different from managing army draftees or schoolchildren—compulsion may bring them into the organization, but compulsion alone is insufficient to make them productive members of it.

The recruitment of valuable FBI informants is no different. Though I do not have equally detailed data on FBI informants, the testimony of FBI agents is consistent with the pattern described above. Informants are very important to making cases against auto-theft rings, and according to the supervisor of a squad handling such cases, "most of our informants have been caught and flipped" or are otherwise "in a bind." Sometimes the FBI agent will promise to "put in a good word" with the prosecuting attorney, sometimes he will agree to overlook minor criminal activities, usually he will pay them small sums of money. But if the generalizations of these agents are accurate, the FBI compared to the DEA recruits more informants with money than with leniency.

One reason may be that the FBI has more informants than the DEA, not only because its jurisdiction is far wider but because FBI agents, unlike DEA agents, do not generally work undercover.[13] If information is to be obtained from criminal sources without arousing suspicion, the informant and not the agent will have to do it.

But another, and more important, reason is that the FBI requires a lower net incentive to recruit an informant than does the DEA, and thus small sums of money will achieve in the former organization what only the threat of prosecution will produce in the latter. The reason is simple but of utmost importance: the FBI does not require its informants to testify in court, unless they are defendants in the case; the DEA typically does. In investigative parlance, DEA agents will "burn" their informants but FBI agents will not. The risks to an FBI informant—from criminal reprisals, from peer-group rejection—being less, the price he can exact is lower.

The FBI is quite firm about its policy of never burning an informant except in the most unusual cases and then only with the informant's permission and after high-level Bureau review. The supervisor of an FBI squad specializing in organized crime told an interviewer that "we [the Bureau] will guarantee an informant's anonymity—we'll even throw away good cases to protect him." A dramatic example is the Hotel

Pierre robbery in 1972. Though the case was solved and the perpetrators arrested because of an FBI informant, the FBI refused to divulge his identity or to produce him in court. As a result, the case against the robbers became quite shaky. Two members of the Pierre gang eventually went to prison, but for terms far shorter than their crime might have warranted; a third was not prosecuted at all. The FBI's position was that the informant's appearance in court would destroy the usefulness of a man who was providing valuable information in several other important cases.[14] Furthermore, the Bureau believes that its guarantee of absolute anonymity is essential to the recruitment of future informants—"what we have going for us," one agent said, "is that people know they can trust us."

That the DEA is prepared to have its informants testify in court reflects the difference between the instigative and the investigative tasks. The FBI, since it investigates cases based on victim complaints, expects, not unreasonably, that an informant can be used primarily to identify suspects or locate loot and that other investigatory methods can be used to supply the confirming evidence—having the victim identify the culprits or the loot, finding physical evidence (such as fingerprints), or placing the suspects under surveillance so as to catch them in the act of committing a new crime. But the DEA has no complaining victims—the only witnesses to the crime are those who are parties to it, and thus there is no innocent person to testify except for the agent himself should he participate in, or observe, the transaction. Nor is physical evidence likely to be of much value; unfortunately, all heroin, unlike all automobiles or jewels, looks pretty much alike, and fingerprints will not be found on powders.

If all the DEA were interested in were street-level drug transactions, the absence of a victim, of physical evidence, or of an informant would be no bar to prosecution. All that would be necessary would be for the agent to make an undercover buy and then arrest and testify against the seller.

And in fact many DEA arrests are precisely of this sort. But DEA agents would like to prosecute the members of a criminal organization that carry out many transactions, most of which are never observed. To identify the members of this organization, an informant is necessary; to convict persons who supply street-level dealers, the testimony of these dealers is necessary. There must, of course, be corroborating evidence—the unsupported testimony of an informant-accomplice is rarely adequate. Such evidence can be obtained by making large-scale buys and seizures, or by building conspiracy cases with information as to the conversations and meetings among suspected violators.

The more important the case, the more likely it is that the informant's testimony is needed. But the more important the case, the greater the potential risk to the informant-witness. Thus, the greater the incentive the would-be informant must have to testify.

Manipulating the threats and opportunities facing a would-be informant so as to produce a net incentive sufficient to induce him to cooperate becomes a key skill of a narcotics agent. The ultimate cost to the informant is, of course, being killed in reprisal for his cooperation. DEA agents believe this is not a trivial possibility—one, in charge of informant records at a DEA office, said "three or four" informants in that region had been killed in the preceding six months. A supervisor in that office estimated that "at least twelve" had been killed in the preceding five years. Still, death is not the normal reward for the snitch. I reviewed the records of a random sample of forty-three informants who had been recruited in 1972 but who, by 1974, had been deactivated. Of the forty-three, *none* had been killed and only two were known to have quit under clear threats of harm. Most were dropped from the active roster because they had provided no useful information or had lied (twelve), because they had moved away or otherwise failed to make contact (fifteen), because they had been immobilized by being imprisoned or deported (seven), or because they had completed their job and were of no further use (six). If these data and the testimony of street agents are any guide, the odds in favor of an informant surviving are reasonably good.

That in itself is a striking fact. One might suppose that heroin traffickers, being serious and ruthless criminals with a great deal to lose, would easily become suspicious of a possible informant, would go to great lengths to investigate his loyalty, and would not hesitate to injure or kill a defector. Such, certainly, are the hazards portrayed by television dramas about the underworld. In fact, the world of street dealing is so localistic and the number of groups and organizations active on the street so large that a dealer can defect in one place and, by moving a few blocks away, resume business in another. Much, of course, depends on the level of the dealer and what is asked of him.

A low-level street dealer is usually asked only to identify his supplier ("connection") and to introduce ("duke in") an undercover agent. No testimony is required. The reward is a reduced or dismissed charge on the original violation. The risks can be kept manageable in a number of ways. One is to double-duke in a second agent so that the original informant can claim he never knew the agent who finally made the arrest. Another is to allow the passage of time. If an arrest follows by several weeks or even months the original duke, the arrested supplier is likely to forget who introduced him to the undercover agent. A third is simply to lie. The informant can claim he was unaware that the person he introduced to the supplier was an agent. As one experienced and successful black agent told an interviewer:

> All the informant wants is not to testify. Anything else, they can con their way out of it. . . . Most crooks don't remember who introduced them to the agent anyway. And if they do, the informant can con out: "Hey, I didn't know he was The Man!"

This agent was especially skillful at keeping his informants out of court, and he benefited from the reputation that gave him. As he said, "Word gets around if you don't burn 'em, and they'll work for you." Another agent always tried to arrange to get corroboration of large undercover purchases by surveillance so as not to need informant testimony.

But many times the informant must testify if there is to be a case. On the very largest cases, this may mean relocating the informant under a new identity. On not so large cases, however, the agency may not be able to afford or to arrange such complete protection. In these instances, the informant-witness must fear not cooperating with the agents more than he fears his former accomplices. The only fear the agents can supply is the credible threat of an unacceptably long prison term.

Many agents believe that judges have given low-level dealers such lenient sentences as to weaken significantly the agents' bargaining power. It is quite possible, as one agent said, that a "dealer will fear reprisals much more than three to six months in jail." There are (as of 1977) no mandatory minimum sentences for drug dealing in the federal statutes, and thus a judge is free to give as low a sentence as he feels inclined. We saw in chapter 2 that the probability of going to prison on a sentence of three years or more if convicted of dealing in narcotics is only .46 despite the fact that United States attorneys usually accept for prosecution only cases involving fairly large dealers. The *convicted* dealer has better than one chance in two of getting off with less than a three-year sentence, which means with less than eighteen months of actual time served. (His chances of a three-year sentence if prosecuted in federal court are only one in three.) Some agents deal with this problem by threatening to prosecute under state law if by that they increase the chances of a prison term. In New York State, for example, the so-called "Rockefeller Drug Laws" mandated long sentences for certain classes of dealers and DEA agents in New York would, in consequence, sometimes threaten a dealer with "going the state route."

Plea bargaining is of utmost importance to narcotics agents. Without a chance to haggle over the kind of offense charged (simple possession, possession with intent to sell, selling various quantities) and over the penalty, there would be little chance to "flip" a defendant other than with payments (which, without plea bargaining, would probably have to be large) or by appealing to motives of vengeance or sympathy. Narcotics agents in this country are placed in a difficult position: favoring high mandatory minimum sentences for drug dealing, both on grounds of just deserts and to provide a credible sanction, and requiring flexibility in sentencing in order to consummate whatever bargains can be struck.

Efforts to flip a suspect begin almost with the moment of his arrest. The critical period is the hours between his being taken into custody and his formal arraignment. In this period, his uncertainty is greatest and his defenses the lowest. In one arrest I witnessed, two young men accused of smuggling large amounts of cocaine into the United States from South America were picked up in the home of one of their parents. The mother was distraught and the young men were solicitous of her welfare. During the automobile ride and in the DEA office where they were searched, photographed, and fingerprinted, the agents told them that there was a "hard way and an easy way to do this." The hard way was to remain silent and face charges; the easy way was to name their suppliers and accomplices and "get a break." No specific break was mentioned, nor could it be, since the agents do not control the prosecutor's or the judge's discretionary authority, but the suggestion, while nonspecific, was clear. The maximum penalties the suspects faced were frequently mentioned. They were allowed to telephone a friend or attorney, but, as the arrest was made at night, there was little chance of seeing an attorney before morning. After one or two hours of processing, the suspects were taken to the federal detention center and locked up. The following day, the agents met with the assistant United States attorney to discuss the case and to enlist him in the effort to flip the accused. He was cooperative, but after a day or so of negotiating with the suspects' lawyer, it became clear that no deal was going to be made. The agents were disappointed, since they wanted the source more than they wanted the importers, but not surprised: "You either flip 'em right away, or you don't flip 'em at all." But they decided to keep trying as the case slowly worked its way up to a trial date. If bail could be set high enough, remaining in jail while awaiting trial could create an additional inducement to flip in order to get out. But bail was met, the importers were freed, and hopes for a flip vanished.

Another arrest had a more productive outcome. A large-scale heroin dealer was jailed to await trial after having been busted by an undercover agent. As it happened, his wife had just given birth and the agents were able to convince him that, as one later put it, "he wouldn't see his daughter until *she* had a daughter—we were talking twenty-five years." None of his accomplices came forward to bail him out. Finally, he decided to flip and become a witness for the state. His testimony, corroborated by other evidence, resulted in the conviction of an entire distribution system, the major figure of which received two consecutive twenty-year sentences. The charges against the witness were dismissed and he was given a new identity in another state.

Developing and controlling informants are subject to many procedural but few substantive rules. To "establish" a (Class I) DEA informant, the recruiting agent must place on file a name and description, a photograph and set of fingerprints, and a brief criminal history. A code number is assigned to the informant. Unless absolutely essential, women and drug users are not recruited as informants, persons under the age of eighteen must have parental consent, and persons on parole must have the permission (not always granted) of their parole officer. The FBI has comparable rules, and in addition requires that copies of the files on informants be sent to Bureau headquarters and that agent contacts with informants be made on a regular basis. Whereas DEA regional directors can authorize the payment of funds ("P/I," or purchase of information) to informants, FBI special agents in charge of field offices can only do so up to certain small limits; to go beyond those amounts requires headquarters approval.

Not only does the FBI have somewhat more centralized procedural controls over informant use than does the DEA, for years it attempted to maintain a large number of informants by having quotas that each street agent was expected to meet. In one field office, the quota at the time was three potential criminal informants (PCIs) and one criminal informant (CI) per agent. The special agent in charge (SAC) of the office took the enforcement of the quota seriously because his management had been criticized by inspectors from headquarters for, among other reasons, an inadequate number of informants. The SAC spoke to those agents who were below the quota and a flurry of activity resulted. Within a short period of time, the number of PCIs established by the office increased by 117 percent while the number of CIs increased by 6 percent.

The differences in these rates of increase suggest the relative ease with which PCIs could be found and the much greater difficulty of converting, in accordance with Bureau standards, a PCI into a bona fide CI. One FBI agent described to an interviewer how he responded to the enforcement of the quota:

> I was called in for a little pep talk by the SAC. . . . I went out and found this former CI and reopened him in order to get the stat [i.e., statistic]. This guy's been opened and closed a half dozen times in this office. He hasn't given me any leads yet but I probably have a year in which to get something from him. I got the stat, but I didn't really improve the office.

By 1977, the Bureau had abandoned the PCI category and thus the opportunity for assigning quotas for it.

The DEA has not had a quota for informants, nor, at the

time of this study, did it maintain at headquarters any central records on informants. Given the nature of its cases, quotas are scarcely necessary: without an informant, few cases can be made at all, and thus the DEA can monitor its agents' performance by examining case output or undercover buys without worrying about how many informants have been recruited.

Though there are in both agencies a number of procedural rules governing informants, neither agency controls or analyzes in any detail how agents utilize informants. In the DEA, for example, there was not at the time of this study any systematic effort made to review cases and arrests to ensure that all potential informants had been developed or to manage the use of existing informants to ensure that they were optimally deployed. Indeed, until the research for this study was undertaken, the DEA had almost no data on how informants were recruited and used. Recently, this has begun to change: supervisors now are supposed to review informants periodically.

In one local office, the two hundred thirty-four arrests made during one year (1972) led to the development of eleven new informants as of mid-1974. Another sixty-one informants came from other law enforcement agencies and various nonarrest sources. The productivity of arrests, measured by the proportion that resulted in informants, was low—less than 5 percent. And the fertility of the informants that were recruited was not high. The seventy-two informants identified one hundred three subjects who were liable for arrest on drug charges; of these new arrestees, only six became informants. Of the six new informants, only one produced a lead to a new informant. Thus, the fertility rate of the first cohort of informants was only 8 percent and that of the second cohort 17 percent. Whether these results could or should be improved upon is a matter of judgment; what is striking is that, despite the critical importance of informants to the work of narcotics agents, the administrative apparatus of the DEA has not traditionally devoted much attention to the matter.

The resources devoted to paying informants are not large. In the calendar year 1975, just over $2 million was spent on P/I—the purchase of information—or about $1,260 for each of the 1,700 agents in the field. (The FBI spent about $3.5 million on informants in the same period.) Much more money—over $5.6 million—was spent on P/E—the purchase of evidence (or undercover buys). Depending on the year, between two thirds and three fourths of the available confidential funds are spent on making buys rather than acquiring information. Most of the P/E funds are never recovered.

What the appropriate ratio should be is a subject of dispute within the DEA. Many agents and supervisors believe that the best way to make cases against entire criminal organizations is to invest heavily in informants who are then left in place, rather than burned, in order to gather intelligence about distribution systems that can then be made the basis for conspiracy cases. Other agents and supervisors are convinced that every important case must begin with an undercover buy, an arrest, and efforts to flip the defendant so as to implicate the next higher level in the distribution system. There is, in short, a debate between those who would like to see the DEA behave more like the FBI (paid informants left in place who then supply leads for conspiracy cases) and those who believe that drug enforcement requires working one's way up the chain through the buy-bust-flip strategy.

Of late, an effort has been made by some DEA administrators to shift the expenditure of confidential funds toward the purchase of information and away from the purchase of evidence as a way of encouraging informant development. In the Los Angeles office, for example, only 35 percent of the PE/PI money expended during the second half of 1975 was spent to buy drugs while 65 percent went to buy information. But Los Angeles remains the exception: in most of the other domestic regional offices, the great bulk (in Boston and New York, over 85 percent) of the confidential funds are spent on drug purchases.

DEA informants are used primarily to help make arrests or obtain convictions. Even though, as explained earlier in this chapter, an informant is typically essential to any drug arrest, not all informants have to be used to make arrests. Yet with only occasional exceptions informants are not used for strategic purposes.

Some of the reasons have to do with the nature of the informant rather than the inclinations of the agents. "You are always at the mercy of your informant" is a familiar phrase among narcotics agents. Every agent would like to wrap up an entire distribution system, but it is the rare informant who will make this possible. Defendant-informants are usually not trustworthy persons. While they may promise to give up important drug suppliers, they have every reason to give up as little as possible—by minimizing their disclosures, they minimize the risk to themselves, reduce the likelihood of harming a friend or close associate, and leave open the possibility of going back into business with their old connections once the heat is off. And informants have an interest in giving up not their own suppliers but rival dealers and other competitors.

About the only way to test the reliability and value of an informant is to make undercover buys and an arrest. Then, at least, you know the significance of the information you have bought. To leave an informant in place in a criminal organization over a long period of time is to deny oneself the opportunity to test the validity of his information or to lose control over him altogether. Intelligence organizations handling double agents face the same problem, but at least they have a few other ways of assessing the reliability of the information obtained: photo reconnaissance, electronic intercepts, published accounts of military deployments, and so forth. Narcotics agents rarely have such checks on informant reliability, for the targets of their efforts are not merely, as with the Soviet Union, remote and secretive, but small and illegal as well. Furthermore, intelligence organizations, operating in the relatively normless world of international intrigue, can control double agents by the threat of extreme sanctions (violence, death, or exposure) that are denied to law enforcement organizations operating under the inspection of the courts and public opinion. Finally, intelligence agencies can deploy their own agents under deep cover in foreign governments without having to fear that this will oblige the agents to perform unacceptably immoral acts— they will be, after all, working in entirely legal, though foreign, government bureaus. The DEA could not place its own agents into a narcotics distribution system unless it was prepared to allow the agents to buy and sell illegal drugs and perhaps to engage in illegal violence. Not only is such behavior against the law, it would also be morally repugnant to most agents.

These difficulties do not rule out entirely the possibility of using informants to produce strategic and conspiracy-establishing, as opposed to tactical and bust-inducing, intelligence. Occasionally a high-ranking informant can be found who is either trustworthy or controllable. But the agent has few incentives to leave him in place and many to use him for a bust. The agent works in a group setting in which the most dramatic and rewarding activity is the chase and the bust. In this environment, he proves himself by his ability to develop a case to the point that a bust accompanied by a substantial drug seizure is possible. Those who spend their time talking on the telephone, shuffling papers, or "going along for the ride" do not acquire prestige. As one experienced supervisor put it: "Narcotics agents are a certain kind of animal—door-kicking heroin agents. Other agents think there is something wrong with a guy who will pass up tonight's buy."

The data compiled by DEA administrators reinforces this

inclination. Each local office must report regularly the number of arrests and the amount of drugs seized for each kind of drug and level of violator. By classifying violators from I to IV on the basis of their importance in a distributional system, the reporting system seeks to encourage making high-level cases. But since high-level cases are very difficult to make, the practical effect of the reporting system is to encourage agents to believe that they are being evaluated by the number of busts and seizures. As one agent told an interviewer:

> My concern is over the numbers game. Supervisors and regional directors are always putting pressure on you for numbers—arrests, seizures, buys. . . . So the agents [in this office] are having to make shitbum street buys of spoons of heroin in order to produce the stats. . . . In our evaluation reports, all they care about is the number of undercover buys. That can be meaningless. Surveillance and so on doesn't count.

The first-line supervisors are quick to deny that they are in "the numbers game." Their interest in high-level cases, they say, is as great or greater than that of the agents. But the agents find it "too easy" to make low-level buys and arrests and are thus reluctant to invest the time in the slow and patient development of larger cases. The statistics, such as the G-DEP (the geographic drug enforcement program) reporting system, are not, in the eyes of supervisors, very important—as several said to interviewers, "It's probably mostly for Congress."

While the DEA has very few intelligence (or "strategic") informants, the FBI has had many. Between 1965 and 1975, according to an estimate by the General Accounting Office, about one fifth of the FBI's investigative matters pertained to intelligence,[15] involving both "domestic security" (individuals and organizations that, in the view of the Bureau, seek to overthrow the government of the United States, advocate the use of violence, or act to deprive others of their civil rights) and "foreign counterintelligence" (directed against individuals and organizations working covertly on behalf of foreign powers).

At one time, domestic security cases commanded a substantial fraction of Bureau resources. One or more squads devoted to these matters existed in every field office, each reporting to the Internal Security branch of the Intelligence Division at headquarters. In 1974, 157 separate organizations were under investigation by the FBI, including most elements of the radical left (such as the Communist Party, Socialist Workers' Party, Students for a Democratic Society, Weather Underground), and other organizations, not Marxist, that the FBI considered "extremist" (such as the Black Panther Party, the Symbionese Liberation Army, the Nation of Islam or "Black Muslims," the Ku Klux Klan, the American Indian Movement, and the National Socialist White Peoples' Party).[16] Not all organizations were equally subject to scrutiny. The Bureau distinguished between those, such as the Communist Party or the Black Panthers, in which both leaders and rank-and-file members were objects of full investigations, those, such as the American Nazi party or the Black Muslims, in which only leaders were fully investigated, and those, such as the Ku Klux Klan, in which there is a full investigation of everyone present at meetings at which possibly illegal acts are discussed.[17]

At the high point of the domestic security effort in the early 1970s, the FBI had between 1,000 and 1,700 domestic security informants.[18] The recruitment and use of these informants raise some of the most difficult problems facing an investigative agency and, in the case of the FBI, have led to some serious abuses of government power, some substantial investigative successes, and a large number of activities the merits and legitimacy of which are and will always be controversial.

Obviously, it is almost impossible for an outside observer to learn much about the use of intelligence informants. However, some revealing glimpses into both the value and the costs of such programs can be gleaned from Senate hearings at which erstwhile informants testified. In June 1973, one Mary Jo Cook, a graduate student living in Buffalo, was recruited by the FBI as an informant to report on one faction of Vietnam Veterans Against the War (VVAW).[19] Her motives were both financial (she was paid about $300 a month and helped in finding a job) and, apparently, altruistic—the agent persuaded her that by working for the Bureau inside VVAW she could help prevent well-meaning persons from being manipulated by subversive influences and could exercise a modicum of restraint on what might otherwise become an extremist organization. But there was also the excitement of the task. Ms. Cook was later to tell the Senate subcommittee that "it was more exciting working as an informant than working as a teller in a bank," another job she held at the time. "I found working as an informant a much more satisfying lifestyle and involvement."[20] In time, however, she became disillusioned with her role as she came to identify with the goals and stance of VVAW and to become an outspoken opponent of the Vietnam war. She quit as an informant a year and a half later, in November 1974.

Gary Thomas Rowe, by contrast, never came to dislike the FBI, especially his contact agents, or to identify with his target organization, the Ku Klux Klan.[21] An FBI informant in the Klan from 1959 to 1965, he finally surfaced (was "burned") when, atypically, he testified in court, in this case against those Klan members who had killed Viola Liuzzo, a woman from Detroit who had helped civil rights activists in Alabama. For six years before this, Rowe reported on Klan activities in and around Birmingham and on the close, cooperative relationship between the Klan and key members of the city police, the sheriff's department, and the local judiciary. Initially, he was told not to participate in any violent acts but in time did join in mob beatings of blacks after having told his contact agent what was scheduled to happen. The agent, obviously, was on the spot: if Rowe observed the law and did not participate, his status as an informant might be compromised; if he joined the mob, he would contribute to injuries inflicted on innocent persons.

According to Rowe, the Bureau said that "we have to by law instruct that you are not to participate in any violence" but that the "important thing" is to "get the information."[22]

Later, Rowe claims he was instructed to participate in that phase of "COINTELPRO" aimed at the Klan. COINTELPRO, or the counterintelligence program, was a policy of disruption and harassment aimed at certain organizations deemed subversive, violent, or extremist. Usually, it involved FBI agents sending false and anonymous letters to organization members or to employers and newspapers designed to discredit a leader or his organization or to stimulate factional quarreling.[23]

These two cases are probably not representative of all domestic security informants, but they illustrate some of the problems the program encountered. One was later called the "vacuum-cleaner problem" and arose because of the widely understood expectation among FBI agents that the maximum amount of information was desired on all organizations that might possibly qualify as subversive, violent, or extremist. Given the management style then in force, it was a far worse sin to say "I don't know" in response to an inquiry from headquarters about a group than to gather intelligence about entirely innocent or at least benign organizations. In the FBI, what you don't know *can* hurt you, at least bureaucratically.

A second problem is that of illegal informant actions. Should the Bureau always prevent if it can, and punish if it cannot, the criminal actions of a valuable informant? In 1976, the Bureau and the Department of Justice came to grapple with this issue by devising guidelines to cover such matters, but no guidelines can do much more than restate the law and urge officials to obey that law and, in the gray areas, to use their judgment. It was of course illegal for Rowe to beat Birmingham citizens and it is illegal—a misprision of felony—for any person, "having knowledge of the actual commission of a felony cognizable by a court of the

United States," to conceal and not make known as soon as possible to a judge the fact of that felony.[24] But the strict application of such rules might render it impossible for the FBI to maintain any informant among the ranks of organized crime or groups, such as the Klan, that regularly employ violence or otherwise break the law.

The attorney general's instructions to the FBI on the use of informants illustrate this dilemma. Informants are not to commit acts of violence, use unlawful methods to gain information, initiate a plan to commit a criminal act, or participate in a criminal act "except insofar as the FBI determines that such participation is necessary to obtain information needed for the purposes of a federal prosecution." Similarly, if the FBI learns that an informant has violated these rules while carrying out an assignment, it shall "ordinarily" notify appropriate local law enforcement agencies or the Department of Justice.[25] In deciding whether to make this notification, the FBI is to consider various factors (for example, the seriousness of the crime). It is helpful that the use of an informant is now constrained by guidelines, but these must—of necessity—allow discretion to exist and thus must require judgment to be exercised.

A third problem is the use of disruption and harassment. Ms. Cook suspected that the FBI was regularly warning employers against hiring members of VVAW and was even responsible for securing her dismissal from a factory where she worked after resigning as an informant. Rowe was allegedly told to seduce women and to circulate malicious gossip. FBI agents, acting directly rather than through informants, wrote anonymous letters designed to embarrass members of the Klan, the Black Panther Party, and various leftist organizations. One's immediate instinct is to condemn such acts as contemptible, as indeed they are. But that does not cover the matter. Granted that they are dirty tricks, are they always inappropriate applied to any organization under any circumstances? Against the Soviet secret police? Against an illegal conspiracy bent on terrorist bombings, such as the Weather Underground? Against even the Klan, when the federal government lacks legal jurisdiction to arrest and prosecute Klansmen for certain of their illegal acts and local law enforcement agencies are unwilling, out of political sympathy, to take any action themselves? But if there are circumstances in which one might reasonably contemplate authorizing such acts, there obviously should be some effort to define, in the most limiting manner, what those circumstances might be. For most of its history, the Bureau did not devote much effort to that issue.

In general, FBI investigations in the domestic security field have employed routine methods and were designed for purposes of intelligence rather than harassment. Of the 800 or so security cases reviewed by the General Accounting Office, only 1 percent involved mail covers, 1 percent surreptitious entries, 8 percent electronic surveillance, and 4 percent photographic surveillance.[26] By far the most common methods were "pretext contacts" (inquiries of the subject or his associates made by an FBI agent pretending to be someone else, such as a building inspector, lawyer, or customer) and physical surveillance (ranging from spot checks to following a subject). Under COINTELPRO, 2,300 instances of "neutralizing activities" occurred. These typically involved sending false or anonymous letters to subjects or their associates or to the media in order to disrupt the organization.[27] The entries ("black-bag jobs") and "neutralizing" activities were concentrated in the New York field office.

The domestic security effort did not lead, and by and large was not intended to lead, to criminal prosecutions. Only 3 percent of the investigative matters were referred to federal prosecutors, and only half of these actually resulted in a prosecution.[28] All of the cases referred to prosecution involved violations of the ordinary criminal statutes and not of any internal security laws. Domestic security was and is an *intelligence*, not an investigative program. This fact has been well known to congressional committees, the attorney general, and the president for decades, not only because these officials were regularly briefed by the FBI on the results of its intelligence efforts, but because such groups and officials regularly made requests of the FBI for information about particular persons, especially those who were candidates for important federal positions or who were the objects of some official's dislike or suspicion.[29] It was never the Bureau policy to say, "We don't know and can't (or shouldn't) find out."

The use of domestic security informants has been substantially reduced in recent years because of the decision of the attorney general and of Director Clarence Kelley to close out most such cases. Between 1975 and 1977, the number of investigative matters in this area fell from about 10,000 to fewer than 700. More revealing is the number of organizations and individuals under scrutiny. In 1974, 157 groups and an undetermined but very large number of individuals were the objects of a domestic security investigation. By September 1977, only 17 organizations and groups and about 130 individuals were under full investigation. There were comparable decreases in the number of agents and informants being used in this area.[30] The management of these matters was also realigned: all domestic security cases, with the exception of those pertaining to the Communist Party, USA, were assigned to the Investigative Division in an effort to link them more closely to the standards and routines of general criminal investigation. (Communist Party matters were transferred to a counterintelligence unit.) A new unit was created on "terrorist research" in response to a GAO complaint that little effort had been made to analyze the vast amount of intelligence materials gathered.

If a problem for the FBI has been to define the proper scope of informant activity, a problem for the DEA and its predecessor agencies has been to insure that a proper relationship exists between informant and agent. The risk, simply, is corruption. When the BNDD was being created in

1968 out of the old Federal Bureau of Narcotics, a large number of FBN agents were discovered to be engaged in illicit dealings with narcotics dealers. In return for supplying agents with chances to make undercover buys from certain dealers in order to meet the pressure for arrests, informants expected to be protected in their own narcotics dealings. Some agents in the New York FBN office were actually selling heroin. In late 1968, these and other agents were indicted by the Department of Justice; in time, there was a wholesale purge of the office.[31]

When John Ingersoll became the first director of the BNDD, he attempted to minimize the risk of agent corruption by deemphasizing domestic drug arrests. If dealers were not arrested, informants would not be necessary. Instead, Ingersoll favored disrupting distribution systems that were importing heroin from overseas. To that end, he increased the number of agents sent abroad to work with foreign police services, using buy money to make wholesale undercover purchases in Marseilles, Hong Kong, and other drug centers. This strategy—the so-called "systems approach"—did, indeed, reduce the number of drug arrests BNDD made in the United States and thus reduced the risk of agent corruption that arises from recruiting informants.

However, this approach gave rise to problems of its own. For one thing, overseas buys require the use of informants and thus the risk of corruption remains, moderated, perhaps, by the fact that it is easier to keep an eye on agents working a few major traffickers than it is to watch agents dealing with hundreds of street dealers. More importantly, such a strategy means cutting back on federal efforts to enforce the laws of the United States within the United States. This has two adverse consequences, one operational, the other political.

Operationally, domestic narcotics law enforcement is left primarily in the hands of local police agencies, some of which have shown a degree of corruption or indifference un-

matched by anything revealed by FBN or BNDD. Moreover, local law enforcement agencies cannot easily develop
large, intercity or interstate cases. Only the federal government can do that, but such a federal role will inevitably entail the development by federal agents of their own stock of
informants.

Politically, it is quite difficult—in the circumstances of the
late 1960s and early 1970s, it was impossible—for a president or the Congress to accept, or at least to defend, a
federal narcotics strategy that forswears arresting large
numbers of domestic drug dealers. Ingersoll himself discovered this when the Nixon administration in 1972 created a
rival organization—the Office of Drug Abuse Law Enforcement (ODALE)—to do what BNDD was not doing: arresting and prosecuting street dealers. Within a year, Ingersoll
was fired and ODALE combined with BNDD (and parts of
the Customs Service) to create the Drug Enforcement
Administration.[32]

In sum, informants, and organizational procedures designed to develop and use them, are a crucial resource for
investigative agencies. Their use creates risks, but their absence leads to failure. The interaction between investigators
and informants is an important—perhaps the decisive—
aspect of the task of these operators. One would suppose
that so important a relationship would be subjected to the
closest administrative scrutiny or would at least dominate
the day-to-day concerns of administrators. In the next two
chapters, the managerial systems of the FBI and the DEA
will be examined with this question in mind.

CHAPTER

4

Managers

IN THEORY, the central tasks of an organization's operators will be defined for them by managers who specify those actions that are necessary and sufficient for the attainment of the organization's purposes. As Leonard D. White wrote, *"Public administration consists of all those operations having for their purpose the fulfillment or enforcement of public policy."* [1] The test of good administration is whether the means selected will efficiently achieve given ends. [2] Chief among these means is the way in which an operator conceives and carries out his tasks. In an investigative agency, this view of administration implies that the kinds of cases selected for investigation and the techniques employed by the investigators will be subject to careful administrative specification. In deciding whether investigators use their time and other resources efficiently, an administrator will presumably ascertain whether, for a given amount of effort, the maximum number of cases, or the maximum number of cases of a given value, are solved. This, in turn, implies that the quality of cases can be somehow measured so as to ensure that the total value of the cases is maximized for a given level of effort.

In fact, investigative managers above the first-line

group supervisors devote relatively little serious attention to specifying what cases should be investigated, determining what techniques should be employed, evaluating the worth of the cases solved, or assessing the relationship between the cases solved and the official goals of the organization. This is not to say that the administrators are uncaring about the behavior of agents or the attainment of purposes, but only that the nature of the agents' tasks and the realities of organizational constraints do not facilitate, and indeed seriously impede, any efforts to administer "rationally" the essential work of the agencies.

This is not how matters may appear to a casual observer. The FBI and the DEA, in quite different ways, seem to devote substantial resources to managing their agents. The FBI is conventionally thought of, even by its own members, as a highly centralized organization that specifies in great and perhaps excessive detail the way in which its agents are to conduct themselves and their cases. The DEA, on the other hand, is usually described as a highly decentralized organization that gives great freedom to regional directors and, within regional offices, to individual agents to instigate and develop cases but that carefully monitors the results of these investigations with a reporting system (G-DEP) that measures the number and value of cases made.

Indeed, the FBI would seem to be a classic example of an organization relying on a *means-oriented* administrative system, and the DEA a good example of one utilizing a *goal-oriented* system.[3] The former controls the behavior of its subordinates by specifying the procedures they are to follow, the latter by evaluating the results obtained. Were this apparent distinction a real one, it would be possible to compare the two investigative agencies to assess the consequences of each administrative strategy. And to a degree that distinction *is* real: it is true that the FBI has an elaborate and centrally managed set of rules and procedures for controlling agents and that the DEA has evolved the G-DEP system of case evaluation, leaving most personnel controls to the discretion of regional directors. But while the differences in degree of centralized control over personnel are real enough, the differences in the extent to which the organizations manage the central *tasks* of the agents are minimal or nonexistent. The administrative systems described below are changing (some of the more important changes are discussed in chapter 5), and thus this should not be taken as a precise description of the FBI or the DEA today. But for many years, these rules, or something like them, have governed.

Administration in the FBI

The 59 field offices and 516 resident agencies out of which FBI agents work around the country present an obvious challenge to administrators at Bureau headquarters: how to ensure that diversity and discretion are kept within acceptable limits. The "acceptable limits" are very narrow, certainly under the leadership of J. Edgar Hoover and to a substantial degree still today. Administrators at FBI headquarters are determined to achieve as high a degree of uniformity as possible in the actions of their field personnel, and to this end the FBI employs many of the same techniques described by Herbert Kaufman in his study of the Forest Service.[4] These include a rigid insistence on hierarchy ("following the chain of command"), the multiplication of written rules to cover all significant contingencies, the inculcation of a distinctive organizational ethos, a centrally controlled personnel system, frequent transfer of field administrators, and a vigorous program of internal inspections.

Hierarchical forms are preserved absolutely. Virtually

every piece of paper arriving at a field office is addressed to the special agent in charge (SAC), every important piece leaving a field office is signed by the SAC. Every written communication coming to or going from an agent is seen by his group supervisor, and every pending case file is periodically reviewed by the supervisor. The SAC is held totally responsible for the conduct of his field office; any problem, however trivial, that may arise will require an explanation—and often an apology—from him. If an agent wishes to call another office or headquarters, the group supervisor must be informed.

Hierarchical authority is reinforced by written rules, most of which have been codified in the looseleaf *FBI Handbook*, a bulky confidential document issued to every agent and frequently updated. Many of the rules simply explain the criminal statutes which the FBI is authorized to enforce and specify the circumstances warranting FBI action. The *Handbook* gives little guidance, however, as to the priority agents are to assign to cases. On the other hand, the *Handbook* is quite clear about the reporting requirements agents face. The investigation of a major theft is to begin "within the hour," that of a routine theft "the same day" (unless the victim has delayed the report of the crime). If the property stolen is valued at $50,000 or more, it is automatically a major theft and a prompt teletype report must be made to headquarters in Washington, followed by daily teletypes until all immediate leads are exhausted. Thereafter, a weekly "airtel" (a report written in telegraphic form but sent by mail) must be submitted to summarize progress on the case.

Until January 1975, when the rule was changed (much to the relief of the agents), each pending investigative matter had to be "posted" at least once every forty-five days. This meant that a report had to be dictated to a stenographer (agents do not type their own reports, and only recently have they begun to use dictating machines) on every pend-

ing matter, even when, as is usually the case, there were no
developments to report and few prospects of any. When the
headquarters inspection team would arrive, among the first
things they would look for was evidence of delinquencies in
meeting the posting rules. In one field office, a 1973 inspection report found eleven delinquent investigations (i.e., case
files) and five delinquent leads (i.e., requests sent from
other offices). Furthermore, the case supervisors at headquarters reviewed field reports on pending matters that
were delinquent and these were tabulated monthly for each
office. The January 1974 tabulation, for example, found that
delinquencies, as a percentage of all active cases, ranged
from 0.1 percent in Little Rock to 14.0 percent in Minneapolis. Whether the Little Rock SAC was congratulated
on his performance that month is unknown, but there can be
no doubt that the Minneapolis SAC heard about his delinquencies in no uncertain terms.

Rules also cover the use of informants. Though headquarters approval is not required for establishing ordinary
criminal informants, it is for security and "extremist" informants. The rules further specify that each criminal informant must be contacted at least once every thirty days and
every extremist informant once every two weeks. Payments
beyond small sums can only be made after headquarters approval. In general, security and extremist cases have always
been subject to tight central control, and in March 1976, the
attorney general issued guidelines that further defined and
centralized the management of these matters.

The rules in the *Handbook* are enforced by a meticulous
and much-feared system of administrative inspections. The
inspectors—known familiarly to street agents as "the goon
squad"—are a group of officials at headquarters organized
into teams of varying size that, under the Hoover regime,
would descend without warning on a field office. Now, the
local SAC gets ten days warning. Each field office is in-
spected about every year and a half. The teams are headed

by agents who have the rank of inspector (usually, men who have been assistant special agents in charge, or ASACs) and "Inspectors' Aides" (usually, men with experience as group supervisors who are in training to become ASACs). The Inspection Division, recently merged with the Planning Office, is headed by an assistant director of the Bureau who is one of the few division heads reporting directly to the director.

It takes a few weeks to inspect a field office (except for the mammoth New York office). Virtually every matter is reviewed—one quarter to one half of all the pending files, automobile maintenance records, the productivity of the stenographic pool, the physical condition of the office and its technical equipment, the registers on which agents sign in and out while on duty, lists of informants, financial vouchers, agents and office caseloads, the SAC's public relations contacts, employee recruitment efforts (with special attention to minority recruitment), training programs run for local police departments, and so on and on and on. The printed questionnaire sent to the SAC at the beginning of the inspection once ran to forty-three pages of detailed inquiries, many of which required lengthy responses; it has recently been abbreviated.

The purpose of the inspection is to ensure compliance with every Bureau directive. The final report of the inspection team may contain over four hundred pages of remarks, most of them in blunt language. One inspector wrote to a SAC that he was guilty of "slipshod" methods and added, sarcastically, that "it is hoped that it is not an exercise in futility to instruct you to give immediate attention to the logical leads suggested by the previous Inspector." The report will note "substantive errors" in the case files ("logical leads" not followed, investigations unduly delayed, or failure to check the appropriate files) as well as "errors of form" (spelling mistakes, misfiled records, omitted dates or case numbers, or—until 1975—posting delinquencies). Whenever the inspector finds an error or offers a criticism, the SAC is obliged to respond in writing with an explanation (often an apology) and a promise to correct the problem immediately.

Though case files are viewed and comments made on whether all "logical leads" were followed, neither the purpose nor the effect of the inspection, with a few exceptions, is to direct or guide the management of cases. It would be remarkable, indeed, if the postfactum review of a case file could supply such guidance—the inspectors cannot know as much about the case as does the agent who has the ticket and the errors discovered in the written reports are not likely, if corrected, to have much effect on the solution of the case. Sometimes, however, broad categories of crime can be emphasized by the inspectors in ways that lead to more effort being devoted to them. Such has been the result, for example, in the organized crime area. Once the Bureau decided, in the 1960s, to enter this field on a large scale, the inspectors pressed the field offices to develop well-placed informants inside organized crime and to initiate prosecutions. One field office was complimented on its "most gratifying" accomplishments during the year in this field (a dozen convictions, over a hundred pending prosecutions) but was also admonished to "zero in with maximum force" on key organized crime figures and related matters of political corruption, the amount of which in the city in question was, to the inspectors, "illuminating and alarming." Such categorical pressures no doubt contribute to the energy with which a field office pursues these matters, but they do not guide the selection or management of cases within categories.

What the case review can routinely achieve is to audit the statistical accomplishments of the field office. These accomplishments, reported monthly, are convictions, fines, savings, recoveries, and fugitives. A conviction is, obviously, a person convicted in court on charges that the FBI helped develop. A fine is a money penalty imposed by a judge on a convicted offender. A savings is the amount of money the

United States government did *not* have to award to a citizen making a claim (e.g., to be reimbursed for certain disputed costs incurred in fulfilling a government contract). A recovery is the value of a stolen item, such as an automobile, returned to its owner in a criminal case. A fugitive is a person who has fled to avoid prosecution or who has escaped from custody. The figures, tabulated monthly by headquarters for each field office, will show the number of convictions and arrested fugitives, and the amounts of fines, savings, and recoveries for the current month, for the current fiscal year to date, and for the previous fiscal year together with the percentage change (plus or minus) for each category. Within a field office, such data are compiled for each agent.

Every SAC is keenly aware of how his office stands on "the stats." Should he for any reason become neglectful of them, the inspectors will forcefully remind him of their importance. One field office had an especially good year in "making stats," and accordingly the inspectors were able to write that "the increases shown above are most noteworthy." Lest such a rare compliment induce any sense of complacency, the inspectors added the following most explicit reminder: "As you know, to continue this most favorable trend you must continue to assure that especially the statistical [sic] producing classifications continue to receive vigorous investigative attention, aggressive presentation to the United States Attorney, and close supervisory attention."

Every agent has been sensitive to the importance of his contribution to office statistics. As one agent told an interviewer, "Anybody who says stats aren't important hasn't been around long or is lying." Each conviction is "one stat," whether it be a major art theft or the loss of two kitchen appliances from an interstate shipment. "The SAC puts pressure on the group supervisor, and the supervisor on the agents—'get me some stats.'" This agent explained that he had "two stats this year, both little cases," but having them permitted him to spend a lot of time on a case he thought important and interesting.

Since every agent is assigned a large number of cases and since many have little prosecutive potential, the agent must develop his own strategy for handling his caseload to balance the partially competing needs of stats, case importance, and investigative opportunities. One agent described to an interviewer his decision rule: he worked hardest on those cases that were "going somewhere" and were either big or involved leads from other agents. A lead had to receive priority attention because the agent or office from which it had come would complain if there was no response forthcoming. One's own cases, by contrast, could be worked at one's own pace, subject only to the posting rules (now relaxed) or supervisory review. But to afford the luxury of emphasizing the more interesting cases, the agent also had to have, as he put it, "some shit cases with which to cover your ass by making stats."

There is nothing in principle wrong with an administrative system that utilizes statistics. Indeed, in an organization as large and farflung as the FBI, the absence of any quantitative data on what agents were doing would create serious problems. For example, headquarters must determine the number of personnel to be assigned to each field office and resident agency; without data on caseloads, no rational allocation would be possible. The practical question, of course, is whether the statistics employed accurately measure important things. For most of its history FBI statistics did not meet this test.

There have been several problems. The statistics do not distinguish among cases of greater and lesser importance, and thus the caseload of any agent, group, or field office may be numerically the same as that of another agent, group, or office but qualitatively—in terms of resources consumed and results produced—quite different. Furthermore, some of the statistics were almost meaningless. A "savings" can be

recorded though the FBI had only the most tangential relation to the case and the amount claimed to be "saved" was
the difference between the (typically inflated) figure that a
plaintiff initially demanded from the government and the
much smaller figure for which he finally settled.[5] The savings is not real because there was never any realistic chance
of the plaintiff collecting the entire amount of the claim and
because the judge's decision to reduce or deny the award
may have little or nothing to do with the FBI's investigation
or testimony. Even a "recovery" can be misleading. At one
time, the FBI would take credit for the value of a recovered
stolen automobile even though the automobile was found
and returned to its owner by the local police and the FBI's
involvement in the case was limited to gathering information
about the perpetrators who may have moved the car across a
state line. The Bureau of late has deemphasized single-car
cases. At one time, however, agents assigned to auto theft
would call up local police departments in search of recovered cars, which, if it could be shown they had come from
out of state, were listed as "FBI recoveries." Recently, as
will be discussed in the next chapter, steps have been taken
to eliminate the puffery associated with such dubious categories as savings and recoveries.

Even those statistics that are valid measures of FBI behavior, such as the number of convictions obtained, are not
as helpful as they might be for administrative purposes. The
number of convictions is not an inherently interesting figure:
everything depends on the number of *opportunities* for a
conviction. One might calculate a conviction rate—the ratio
of convictions to prosecutions begun, or to cases presented
to the United States attorney, or to investigations initiated
with known subjects, or to all investigations. The FBI does
not compile any of these rates. Instead, it compares the
number of convictions obtained this year with the number
obtained in previous years, a comparison that may indicate
nothing more than the growth in the crime rate or the inge-

nuity of agents in finding cases with which to make stats. Furthermore, obtaining a conviction is not the only, and perhaps not the best, measure of investigative success. One person may be convicted of a bank robbery but his five accomplices may go undetected or get off scot-free; you might argue that such a conviction statistic is less impressive than one that represents apprehending and convicting the sole perpetrator of a bank robbery. And some cases may be solved but in ways that do not permit claiming a conviction—for example, when compelling evidence is developed against a thief who dies, flees the country, or is surrendered to another jurisdiction (a state, the military) for disposition.

Local police detectives use "clearance rates" as a measure of their success. To "clear" a crime is to identify an offender, have sufficient evidence to charge him, and take him into custody.[6] The arrest of one person can clear several crimes, or several persons may be arrested in the process of clearing one crime. The FBI regularly publishes the clearance rates recorded by local police departments for crimes they handle but, except for bank robbery, does not compile, much less publish, any clearance rates for crimes it investigates.

Many criticisms have been made of clearance rates, especially of the ways in which they can be manipulated.[7] But where carefully compiled and audited on the basis of well-defined criteria, these rates can be used as rough indications of investigative success. Such was the case, for example, in an experiment to test innovative detection methods in the Rochester Police Department.[8] The FBI declines to develop clearance rates, though its reasons are not entirely clear. Some administrators believe that such rates would be meaningless because the FBI shares jurisdiction in most of its investigative matters and it would be impossible to allocate clearances between the Bureau and local police efforts. Yet the FBI shares jurisdiction in bank robbery cases, and a solution rate, which takes into account the involvement of other agencies, is regularly compiled. One field office, for example, was strongly criticized by the inspectors for having solved less than 50 percent of its bank robberies when the Bureau-wide average was over 70 percent.

One reason why clearance rates are not used to evaluate agents may be that, if they were, the agents would have an incentive to work only on the cases easiest to solve (to get that kind of "stat") or would find ways of keeping difficult-to-solve cases out of their caseload, perhaps by referring them to the local authorities. The effect of this would be to reduce the total number of convictions, which many FBI executives believe would be detrimental to Bureau interests. On the other hand, if clearances counted, agents might spend more time getting arrested suspects to admit to other, unsolved crimes and thus produce useful information on the extent the arrestees were important multiple offenders or unimportant, one-time losers. And clearance rates, even if not entirely valid as a measure of Bureau efficiency, could nonetheless draw attention to investigative problems.

How this might work is illustrated by the inspection report on one field office. The inspectors found it to have a low bank robbery solution rate, whereupon they devoted twenty-six single-spaced pages to a probing, critical analysis of the deficiencies in the work of the bank robbery squad. They recommended assigning another agent to the squad, utilizing artists' conceptions of suspects, distributing lists of "bait money,"[9] urging banks to install and operate cameras that would film robberies (six cases had been solved that way in one year), recruiting better informants, distributing photographs and fingerprints of suspects more widely among local police, and so on. In fact, within a year or two, the bank robbery squad was revitalized in accordance with these suggestions and its solution rate had gone up. But in the 400 pages of the remainder of the report, there was no comparably useful advice on case management for other crimes, in large part, one suspects, because for no other kind of crime were data available to alert the SAC or the inspectors to problems of low efficiency.

For decades, headquarters supervision of criminal investigation was vested in a General Investigative Division headed by an assistant director who reported to the deputy associate director of the Bureau. This division was divided into four sections, one of which was concerned with general criminal offenses. In this section, about two dozen supervisors were organized into units by type of crime: one unit handled bank robberies, another thefts from interstate shipments and the interstate transportation of stolen property, and so on. These units corresponded to the investigative squads in field offices and in theory were supposed to provide them with functional supervision. In fact, they did little of the sort.

Some of the tasks of these units were necessary. They compiled information about cases and crimes when a public statement on these matters was to be made, advised on the investigative implications of proposed changes in the criminal law, and kept headquarters officials informed on a daily basis of developments in investigations of national significance (such as the Patty Hearst kidnapping).

But the bulk of the Division's work was far more prosaic, consisting essentially of receiving, filing, and reviewing reports on routine cases mailed in from field offices all over the country. The volume was staggering. For just one offense, interstate transportation of stolen property (ITSP), more than 18,000 new matters arrived at headquarters during one year. For each new case, a "tickler" was made out—a card indicating the date the case began, the office of origin, and other essential facts. There might have been as many as 900 active ITSP cases on tickler at any given time. Once a month, all the ticklers for a given office were pulled and the cases checked to see if investigative progress was being made. When the delinquency rule was in effect, a failure to post the case was noted. Occasionally, the headquarters supervisor sent out a tip, information about similar cases elsewhere, and other leads. But by far the most common outgoing message was the "greenie"—a Form 0-9, printed on green paper, that criticized a local office for its handling of a case or for not making progress.

The bank robbery unit had a larger role because of the traditional importance of that crime to the Bureau and the fact that the unit calculated a solution rate. A field office with a lagging solution rate heard about it; as one supervisor put it, "I believe in the chain of command and putting heat on from the top to get them off their butts." In addition, the unit distributed leads, ran seminars on bank robberies, handled requests from the field for using body recorders and polygraphs (lie detectors), approved the use of a stakeout at a bank, and rendered other services. But "putting the heat on" clearly was its dominant function. As another headquarters supervisor put it, the concern is to "make field agents productive—they've got to be out there selling the soup, and this means workloads, priorities."

In the field, this pressure and supervision were seen quite differently. Almost without exception, agents resented them or tried to ignore them. The general view was that headquarters was rarely helpful, and inevitably so—"cases are solved on the street, not in Washington." A group of several agents who had both field and headquarters experience discussed their attitudes toward Bureau case supervision. "Never," said one, "have I seen headquarters help make a case." Another added, "In twelve years in the field, I never got any help from the headquarters supervisor except for memos about crossing the t's and dotting the i's. It's all cover-your-ass stuff." Most agreed that headquarters can help when it mobilizes resources and finds extra agents for big cases; one agent did mention two occasions in which headquarters leads were helpful in solving some civil rights cases. But another agent seemed to express the group's general attitude when he said that "all they [headquarters] care about is form and rules. Make a mistake in a case write-up and you get a greenie back so fast it'll make your head swim."

Even some administrators in the Division were unhappy

with traditional case supervision. "I don't want the supervisors to just pull ticklers," said one key official. "I want them to be thinkers, innovators." They should, he added, become "more substantive, set priorities." We have to "stop playing the numbers game." He wanted his supervisors to become "coaches, not critics," but confessed that he had not yet figured out a way to make that happen. Considering that a case, with only a few exceptions, develops, is investigated, and is made locally, or at best among only two or three field offices, it was never clear what headquarters could do to improve the process. Most investigative work is simply interviewing people, and that can only happen where the people are.

Headquarters could make a difference in one important regard: by making erring SACs and agents rue the day they erred. One senior Bureau official described this as "defensive leadership." A SAC was told to "use your own judgment" on an important matter but then, if something went wrong, headquarters would criticize him for taking action that had not been authorized and was not correct. Some SACs would adapt to this by calling headquarters in advance for instructions on sensitive matters. Rarely were helpful instructions forthcoming—what, after all, can a man in Washington usefully tell a SAC a thousand miles away who is trying to manage a desperate aircraft hijacker? Everything depends on the latter's detailed knowledge of circumstances, personalities, and contingencies and on his ability to make good guesses and sound judgments. In these cases, headquarters would have been "consulted," though with little practical effect except to permit the SAC to deny, should criticism later arise, that he had acted entirely on his own.

In 1977 this structure of pseudo-centralized case management was abandoned and a new Investigative Division created that no longer was to run a tickler system. The Division now consists of two sections, one for personal and property crimes and domestic security matters and the other for organized and "white-collar" crime. The former section is organized into units for personal crimes (kidnapping, extortion, assassinations), property crimes (ITSP, auto theft, crimes on government reservations), fugitives (escapees, bond defaulters, deserters from the armed forces), bank robberies, and domestic security. No longer would each case be followed or erring offices bombarded with "greenies." Instead, the Division would study workloads and manpower assignments and provide training to the field. It would supervise directly only national or special cases and oversee sensitive investigative techniques, such as infiltrating organized crime. The motives for this change, part of a much larger shift in headquarters philosophy, will be discussed in the next chapter.

Of far greater importance than central case supervision in producing uniform responses among field agents is a personnel system that is designed and operated to produce the maximum degree of central control over the selection, assignment, promotion, and discipline of agents. The absolute personal authority wielded by J. Edgar Hoover over his subordinates is so well known, and so amply confirmed by other written sources, as to scarcely require mention here.[10] Even Bureau admirers of Hoover, and there are many, refer half-jokingly to his era as a "reign of terror." The stories of how that authority was used and the efforts agents made to manipulate or adapt to it are legion and a leading topic of conversation whenever two agents, and especially two former agents, meet. A chance or purely ceremonial meeting between an agent or a SAC and Hoover could, depending on the course the conversation happened to take, result in a notation in the man's file that could lead to rapid promotion or immediate demotion, to an assignment to a popular field office (such as San Diego) or to being exiled to the Bureau's "Siberia," such as Butte or Oklahoma City. For all practical purposes, an FBI agent, unlike most federal employees, had no effective civil service protection.

The FBI under Hoover was an example not of bureaucratic but of patriarchal rule. In a bureaucracy, authority and office are allocated and made legitimate by written rules; in a patriarchy, authority and office among subordinates depend chiefly on personal loyalty to the ruler. A bureaucratic executive may have great power, but it will depend on legal norms; a patriarchal ruler exercises power unencumbered by rules and on the basis of personal or traditional authority.[11]

With the death of Hoover, many of the arbitrary or capricious aspects of the director's authority ended and written rules came to replace personal command. The organization became, in Weber's terms, more bureaucratic, which is to say, more regular, more predictable, and consequently more easily challenged by those who believed a rule to be wrong or a practice to be in violation of a correct rule. The personnel system, though now more formalized and stable, remained nonetheless intact as a powerful system for ensuring that agents, and especially administrators, would adopt a Bureau perspective on their work. All personnel decisions are centrally made—no field office makes significant personnel decisions except for the written evaluations prepared annually on each agent. All hirings, assignments, promotions, transfers, and censures are approved—and many are even initiated—at headquarters. Every field office's organization chart must be approved by headquarters; every office's complement of personnel is determined by headquarters.

The practice of disciplinary transfers—of being exiled to Butte for real and imagined offenses—has been abolished, but the threat of a letter of censure or of being called before the inspectors for a violation of procedure or trust remains real enough. The frequent transfer of agents among field offices for reasons having nothing to do with discipline has also been moderated. Under Hoover, a new agent rarely remained in his first office for more than eighteen months before being automatically transferred to a second office to prevent the development of any localistic orientations. An agent was allowed to express a preference for up to three offices, but if he sought a popular one, such as in the Southwest, he was not likely to get it. Under Clarence Kelley, the policy was changed to permit a new agent to remain in his first office for as long as five years so as to reduce the burdens of frequent moving, and the agent's preferences were taken more seriously in assigning him to his next office.

Though the new street agent is now moved about less than in the past, the promotional process remains as arduous as ever. He can advance more or less automatically, unless he blunders, to the grade of GS-13. He cannot go higher than this, however, unless he opts for "administrative advancement," which requires frequent reassignments and transfers. First, he seeks approval to become a "relief supervisor" (filling in for his group supervisor) in the field office. If he does well, he may become a full-fledged group supervisor. Following this, however, he is taken from his field office and sent to headquarters to be a supervisor in one of the investigative divisions. This is done explicitly to give the man a "headquarters perspective" and to lessen or eliminate the natural hostility the field has toward Washington. Next, he will become an inspector's aide in the Inspection Division for about a year, giving him a chance not only to acquire but to enforce the headquarters perspective. By this time he will have become a GS-14 or even GS-15, whereupon he will be sent back to the field as an ASAC. Before long, however, he will be transferred from that office to become ASAC at another office and, if he continues to impress, he will be brought back to headquarters again as a full inspector, where he will serve until a vacancy opens up as SAC in a small field office. If he is fortunate, he may become SAC in a large office as a grade GS-18 and then have a chance to become an assistant director or deputy assistant director in charge of a headquarters division.

In short, to rise above the grade of GS-13 (which means to earn, before step increases, more than $30,000 a year), one must become a creature of headquarters, trained and managed by it, with little chance thereafter to become strongly identified with the field. Operating this personnel and advancement system has been the powerful Administrative Division at headquarters. Its interest is not in solving cases, making arrests, or developing investigative techniques, but in managing the complex details of the personnel and budget system. It has not had a management information system that would inform it about investigative work, and it therefore could not routinely make its judgment of personnel on such grounds. The investigative divisions that attempt to provide central case supervision have little to say about promotions or transfers.

A senior official in the Administrative Division who, like most of his colleagues, had been in that Division for many years, told an interviewer that the "Admin Division was the focal point of running the FBI," because to run it "you have to know how to run the federal personnel system," and this requires "real technicians." And, indeed, the maze of rules promulgated by the Civil Service Commission and the Office of Management and Budget that define authorized appointments ("slots"), correct procedures, financial limits, and reporting systems can only be understood by specialists. In the FBI, these specialists have used their knowledge to become not simply a staff arm of the director but his operating arm—defining and implementing many of the decisions having important substantive impact. Members of the Division admitted to the existence of conflict between them and the investigative divisions and to their distaste for the formation, under L. Patrick Gray, of an Office of Planning and Evaluation (OPE) independent of it. To many field agents, the Administrative Division *is* the Bureau, for it controls most of what they care about—promotions, transfers, and censures. Under Kelley, it was renamed the Finance and Personnel Division in an apparent effort to deemphasize its role as a general administrative unit.

The control exercised by the managers of the personnel system is made easier by the recruitment process for new agents. All are college graduates, though some become clerks in the Bureau while going to college nights, transferring into an agent's class soon after their graduation. At one time heavy preference was given to graduates of law schools and to professional accountants, but few such persons seek a Bureau career now that opportunities for such professionals (unlike during the Depression years, when the Bureau was growing rapidly) are more attractive outside the government. A large part—an estimated 60 percent—of the new agents now come from the military where they have served as officers, often in investigative, security, or counterintelligence work. Three years of appropriate military service will count toward meeting the requirement for postgraduate training or legal/accounting experience. Such recruits have already become familiar with, and even happy with, strict hierarchical controls.

The centralized administrative system of the FBI is strongly defended by its principal managers. The inspectors are aware of the criticisms made of their methods and concerns, but they can point, justifiably, to the fact that no serious problems of corruption or lack of integrity have occurred in the field. Trivial offenses may result in censure or even sterner punishment, but in consequence graver offenses are deterred. The patriarchal authority of Hoover may have been used arbitrarily, but at least it was used: no agent could defy a superior, protect his incompetence or indifference behind the shield of civil service rules, or fail to understand the importance of following national policies. As one senior inspector put it to an interviewer:

> The key to our success, other than integrity and discipline, is central control. Look at DEA—they have a lot of regions. Headquarters doesn't even know what the man on the street is doing unless the regions decide to tell them. Or CIA—it has tunnel vision: if three men are working on the same problem, one may not even be told what the other two are doing. He'll have to leave the room when it is discussed. . . . You've got to run things centrally.

Administration in the DEA

No one in the DEA would deny that it is, compared to the FBI, a highly decentralized organization. As the Bureau of Narcotics and Dangerous Drugs (BNDD), headquarters exerted some influence over the field by requiring that local offices identify "systems" of narcotics distribution and obtain headquarters approval of their designation and investigation. And as this is written (1976), a new DEA administrator is attempting to reestablish a modicum of central control over the regions. But throughout its formative years (1973–76), and to a substantial degree still today, the organization has been highly decentralized.

The United States is divided by the DEA into thirteen large regions, each headed by a regional director. Within each region there may be a number of smaller, district offices. The New York region, for example, includes district offices in Buffalo, Albany, Newark, Westbury, Kennedy airport, and Rouses Point. The regional director is in charge of the region and all the district offices within it. It is as if the FBI had fifteen rather than fifty-nine SACs: forty-five field offices that now report directly to headquarters would report instead to regional directors and thereby become less amenable to central control.

Regional directors (RDs) in the DEA, unlike SACs in the FBI, remain in office for long periods. One reason for this is that the DEA was formed by a merger of the BNDD and parts of the Customs Bureau; in the politically necessary allocation of top jobs, room had to be found for high-ranking Customs officials. They got their share (about six) of domestic regional directorships and, given the delicate state of Customs-DEA relations, tended to keep them. From 1973 to 1976, not a single regional director was demoted or transferred for disciplinary reasons. Beginning in mid-1976, some changes were made; the curiosity and apprehension with which they were greeted by the RDs provided ample evidence of their rarity.

Decentralization did not just happen, it was actively fostered. John R. Bartels, Jr., the first administrator of the DEA, devolved power on the RDs, in part by design and in part as the unanticipated consequence of his own administrative style, one that was not conducive to either rule by terror or systematic management. As a senior official later described it, "under Bartels, policy decisions were regarded by the field as negotiable instruments." Since Bartels was not himself a narcotics agent (he had been a federal prosecutor), he sought to establish his credibility with field agents—the "1811s," after their civil service designator—by deferring to them. The RDs did not report directly to him, but to the assistant administrator for enforcement (at first) or to the deputy administrator (later). The RDs would call headquarters on unusual or major events and were willing to learn what was expected of them, but they did not seek—and generally did not get—detailed instructions on what to do. Their attitude, as a senior official later explained, was expressed thus: "Don't tell me how to suck eggs."

The crucial investigatory resource—buy money—is allocated to the regions to spend as they wish, save for a small portion (about 10 percent) held in headquarters as a central reserve. The amount an informant is to be paid, the size of a flash roll, the sum to be offered for an undercover buy—all these matters are determined locally. For a while, headquarters approval was necessary for a proposed classification of a violator under its reporting system, but approval was forthcoming as a matter of course—headquarters rarely had any information that would permit it to challenge a classification—and in time the authority to make these classifications was delegated to the field, to be reviewed only after the arrest is made.

Fewer pieces of paper flow to Washington from the field

in the DEA than in the FBI. Copies of case reports (on a form called "DEA 6") and of laboratory analyses are sent along, but there are relatively few reporting rules that are enforced and nothing that even faintly resembles the old FBI posting rules. Each region, naturally, struggles to get manpower and other resources and to do well by the various statistical measures of performance, but regions are generally free to pursue these objectives in isolation from each other. The dissemination of leads is not closely monitored by headquarters, and thus one region might with impunity fail to cover another region's tip.

Within the DEA, there is no counterpart, in effect if not in form, to the FBI's Inspection Division or Administrative Division. The oversight functions of the DEA's Office of Enforcement are much less significant than those of the FBI's General Investigative Division. There is an inspection service in the DEA, and at one time it did operate much like its counterpart within the FBI, monitoring compliance with procedures. And as in the FBI, the inspection unit became a source of substantial power for certain headquarters administrators. Andrew C. Tartaglino, long the chief inspector at the BNDD and for a while that at the DEA, was able, by his testimony before a Senate committee, to set in motion events that led to the forced resignation of his superior, DEA Administrator John R. Bartels, Jr. But inspection efforts in the DEA and BNDD have been primarily directed at integrity problems rather than at securing administrative compliance to headquarters rules of the kind obtained by FBI inspectors.

Evaluating DEA field offices from an administrative and enforcement perspective has recently become the task of the Office of Field Evaluation (OFE), a unit of only three full-time persons that borrows additional personnel when making periodic inspections in the field. Compared to the FBI's inspectors, the OFE is more oriented to substantive matters, giving relatively little attention to "errors in form" or minor procedural details. Since it was not created until late 1975, it is too early to assess its impact on operations, but clearly OFE has not been a source of fear and trembling.

Personnel decisions are neither fully centralized nor fully decentralized—government hiring rules preclude any complete devolution of this function to the field, but regional offices in the DEA have their own personnel officer, recruit candidates, and manage many of the disciplinary problems.

Though the DEA personnel system is more decentralized than the FBI's, the personnel and budgetary officers at DEA headquarters exercise disproportionate influence in agency decisions. The Office of Administration was virtually the sole element of organizational stability during the countless reorganizations of DEA headquarters. In part this is because it was headed by a senior civil servant who was both politically skillful and who had excellent relations with key congressional and Justice Department figures, and in part it was because the office had the technical expertise and records necessary to operate the budget and personnel systems in accordance with complex government requirements. Indeed, the two reasons are not unrelated: external forces (Congress, the Civil Service Commission, the Office of Management and Budget, the Justice Department) create, by their procedural requirements, the need for a powerful Office of Administration; an administrator of that office becomes powerful because he can satisfy the demands of these groups. The costs of challenging such a person's power can be great: to override his decisions, to ignore his advice, or to assign his work to someone else is to risk making a serious blunder in accounting for funds, managing a budget, or reassigning an employee, blunders that, unlike a bungled narcotics investigation, are immediately evident to critical outsiders and can involve violations of important laws and rules. Thus, the capacity of the top personnel and budget officer to block change is very great and not easily reduced.

Case review of supervision by headquarters is virtually

nonexistent, although beginning in mid-1976 a new administrator, Peter Bensinger, launched efforts to change that. A
Domestic Investigations Division existed for several years at
headquarters but with little authority and few duties. In
April 1976, that part of the Division concerned with the
work of the regions had one chief and three "coordinators,"
one for each group of five regions. These men frankly admitted they had nothing of importance to do. They prepared
some statistics (which they believed were useless or misleading), reviewed the files of Class I and Class II cases (but only
after an arrest had been made), and answered inquiries from
other parts of headquarters or from the public. The major
cases were reported to headquarters by teletype, but an
official in the division described it as a "stream of paper" producing "no analysis." Another official complained that "we
don't even read the stuff" and reflected enviously on the
"central control" exercised by the FBI. Both recalled nos-
talgically the period when, as the BNDD, the headquarters
desk officers had an "operational" role, especially with respect to interregional cases. Now, the desk officers had become "trivial advocates for the regions."

The past failure of the DEA to supervise centrally the development of cases might be irrelevant, or even desirable, if
headquarters had the ability and inclination to evaluate re-
liably the results of these cases. Such is in fact the purpose of
the G-DEP system. G-DEP was conceived after dissatis-
faction arose over the earlier "systems approach" followed
by the BNDD. Under the systems concept, an effort was
made to identify and immobilize any significant national
and international drug-trafficking organizations. Beginning
in 1969, the BNDD discovered ten major and seventy-five
secondary drug distribution systems. Although it scored
some successes against these rings, by January 1972 all ten
major systems were still operating (though two had been
"severely disrupted").[12] Equally important, the systems approach had come under attack outside the BNDD (see chap-

ter 6). In its place, G-DEP was installed effective July 1, 1972. Individual offenders were classified according to their geographic location, the kind of drug in which they dealt, and their importance as measured by the amount of drugs they produced or distributed. Regional directors were required to submit semiannual "work plans" in which they stated their arrest goals: how many violators of each class they expected to arrest in the months ahead. These goals were to be in accordance with a general DEA policy of allocating 70 percent of the agency's investigative resources to Class I, II, and III violators. At the end of each year, a comparison was to be made between goals and accomplishments.

During the 1974 fiscal year, the DEA set itself the goal of 7,070 arrests, 148 of which were to be of Class I and 430 of which were to be of Class II violators. It in fact produced (together with the Customs Service and the Immigration and Naturalization Service), 10,636 arrests, 338 of which were at Class I and 657 of which were at Class II. In addition, the G-DEP program tabulates the amounts of "drugs removed." For example, during the last half of 1973, the DEA acting alone "removed" 58,749 grams of heroin, 94,177 grams of cocaine, 45,584 pounds of marijuana, and 709,862 dosage units of hallucinogens.

The chief administrative resource, other than exhortation, that DEA administrators can use to induce regional directors to attain or exceed various goals is the allocation of buy money. The total amount can be increased or reduced, the maximum amounts that can be spent on buying evidence as opposed to buying information can be specified, and the desired allocation of these funds among kinds of drugs and classes of violators can be indicated.

In short, the G-DEP system would seem to provide a rational means for evaluating, qualitatively and quantitatively, the results of agent activities, for planning the optimal allocation of resources used by agents, and for changing where necessary the focus of agent efforts.

In fact, hardly anyone in or out of the DEA was happy with the results. Most administrators believe that some way of measuring agent accomplishments is needed, but few are convinced that the G-DEP system supplies that need. "It's better than a gut reaction," said one headquarters official, lamely. In the field, G-DEP is, with a few exceptions, regarded as a problem rather than an answer. Said one group supervisor, "It's a game, it's public relations. . . . I guess it's OK if it helps in Washington, and at least it doesn't get in our way here."

The problems with G-DEP are in part the problems that would exist with any effort to measure the number of violators arrested classified by their "importance." Most—over 90 percent—of the persons arrested are Class III or Class IV violators. Persons critical of the DEA use that figure to argue that DEA agents are wasting their time on small fry; persons supportive of the DEA explain that a Class I or II violator can only be approached by first arresting his Class III or IV subordinates, who can then be used to implicate the higher-ups or who, if taken out of circulation in sufficiently large numbers, would immobilize a distributional system. G-DEP figures are not compiled in a way that would permit one to choose among these views. The DEA mission is, as it explains it, to bring to justice "organizations, and principal members of organizations" involved in illicit drug trafficking.[13] But G-DEP does not tabulate organizations; it tabulates individuals who may or may not be related organizationally.

One effort to find out whether Class III and IV arrests did or did not lead to the arrest of top violators was made by a DEA headquarters team in the Los Angeles region in 1974. The survey found that 74 percent of the region's PE/PI money was used for Class III and IV investigations but that this money, when expended, resulted "in the arrest of Class III violators, and little else. . . . It was rare that a violator of higher class was arrested, or even identified."[14] In short, the theory that agents "work their way up" the distributional chain by starting with the small fry seemed to be disproved, at least for this region: "cases begun at the Class III level ended at the Class III level."[15]

This result did not occur because DEA administrators wanted that result. Quite the contrary: from the administrator down, DEA officials have repeatedly and emphatically said that the agent's goal is to arrest the big dealers and break up the large organizations, leaving street dealers and other small fry to local police departments or to federal-local task forces. Furthermore, the agents themselves share this goal—few feel they are doing their job if they arrest someone selling a few bags of heroin, and all would welcome a chance to catch a major importer or a kilo dealer (see chapter 2). The Los Angeles region survey included interviews with agents and supervisors which led the authors of the report to say that these operators "all understand that the goal of the Drug Enforcement Administration is the elimination of narcotic traffickers at the highest levels of the traffic." My own interviews with agents in three field offices fully confirm this.

A paradox. An administrative system carefully designed to achieve a goal that is explicitly stated and widely shared in fact seems to produce behavior that is inconsistent with that goal. How can this be explained?

One answer is that, were one to have a complete understanding of the drug enforcement process, there might be no paradox at all. While it is true that only rarely does the arrest of a Class III violator lead to a Class I or Class II arrest, the key question is what proportion of Class I and Class II violators are apprehended as a result of investigative efforts that began with, or at some stage necessarily involved, the arrest of Class III or IV violators. Finding a street-level dealer able and willing to testify against or introduce an undercover agent to a high-level trafficker is a chancy enterprise. When making an initial contact on the street, an agent usually has no way of knowing whether it will lead to bigger things; the odds are it will not. But if the agent has no other source of leads, he must pursue the contact even if the odds are over-whelmingly against it proving productive. The alternative is to do nothing at all. Thus, it is not interesting to know that 75 percent, or even 95 percent, of all arrests are at the Class III level, or that 85 and 90 percent of such arrests lead nowhere. As explained in chapter 2, catching a major nar-cotics dealer is difficult and rare. A low-level dealer may fear reprisals if he cooperates with an agent; a high-level dealer can refuse to do business with an unknown person or even to handle drugs at all; wiretaps are costly and increasingly traf-fickers avoid talking business on the telephone.

There are, in short, perfectly reasonable grounds for thinking that the criticisms of Senate investigating commit-tees and the General Accounting Office are at best in-conclusive and at worst mistaken. What is striking is that although the results obtained by the DEA may be defensible, so little systematic effort is made to defend them. Hardly any resources are devoted to finding out how big cases get made or what the relationship between Class I and Class III arrests really is. There are many reasons, but one of special importance: DEA administrators are almost all career nar-cotics agents who began on the street. To them, statistics are either meaningless or perverse. They did not make cases with their help and they do not believe that either the na-ture of case-making or the value of the results obtained can be measured statistically. To them, statistics have only pub-lic relations value, if that. In some sense, they may be quite right. But as administrators they also know they must be able to report on their results, and G-DEP represents their best effort. It is intended to meet both the need for some management tool and the need for a public accounting.

The system gives them the worst of both worlds. It leads agents to suppose that statistics count and that arrests must be maximized whatever their value. Regional directors look upon it as the basis on which headquarters will decide how many resources each region will get. As the Los Angeles region survey expressed it, "They [agents] viewed routes of advancement within DEA to be open to them predicated on the number of arrests they made and the amounts of narcotics they seized."[16] The regional directors saw G-DEP as the standard by which personnel, funds, and credit were allocated to the regions. Though each would like to take credit for a Class I case, these are not common and some regions, and many offices within a region, have few opportunities to even begin such an investigation. This would be the case, for example, if the top heroin suppliers for a region all lived outside the region. If an RD cannot easily increase his claim on organizational resources by producing many Class I or II cases, he will do the next best thing and increase his claim by pressing for more Class III cases. Finally, G-DEP gives external critics of the agency an excellent weapon to use against it.

A management task force at DEA headquarters came to much the same conclusion: the G-DEP system "may have the effect of condoning a subtle 'numbers game' with each Region striving for a greater number of arrests instead of quality cases having significant impact."[17] To the extent that this is true, the consequences for drug enforcement are serious. Many drug distribution networks cut across regional lines. One organization may bring brown heroin from Mexico into Detroit, where it is cut and then sent on to Boston or New York to be sold on the street. Six DEA regions have an interest in this case: region 15 headquartered in Mexico City, regions 11 (Dallas) and 14 (Los Angeles), with responsibilities along the Southwest border, region 6 based in Detroit, and regions 1 (Boston) and 2 (New York). If agents and regional directors believe they are rewarded for their stats, they will have an incentive to keep leads and informants to themselves in order to take credit for a Mexican heroin case should it develop. A more appropriate strategy would be for such information to be shared so that an interregional case can be made, for one region to take the lead on the case with support from the others, or for the case to be developed by personnel operating out of headquarters independently of the regions. The perceived evaluation and reward system of the organization works against each of these three alternatives because each threatens to lessen the credit, and therefore (it is believed) the resources, available for a given region.

Regional competition for credit and the apparent link between stats and resources does not fully explain the apparent frequency of low-level arrests by DEA agents. Even where both major as well as minor violators can be found entirely within a single region and where no interregional cooperation is necessary, the G-DEP results are about the same. And the agents, unlike the RDs, have little interest in whether their RD gets more or less credit from headquarters. Furthermore, agents make Class III cases even when RDs go to great lengths to persuade them to make bigger cases. One reason is that making bigger cases is very difficult; it takes more than persuasion or incentives to arrest a top heroin dealer. The essential technology of narcotics investigations does not lend itself to major changes in productivity. But in addition, the agent works in a *group* setting in which status is allocated and other intangible rewards provided by his colleagues. In every enforcement group there are a few agents who are known as "street-wise" and productive and others who are seen as "just along for the ride." To get a reputation as being street-wise, one must work effectively undercover; the best evidence that one can do this is one's ability to make buys, develop snitches, and make arrests. If all that one's technology permits is a Class III arrest and seizure, then that is the arrest and seizure one must make if one is to develop a good reputation. One could, in theory, drop a case if it appeared it was not "going anywhere"—no Class I or II violator in sight—but that would mean forfeiting the opportunity to produce any credible evidence of one's ability. Furthermore, every regional office has more than one enforcement group. A group that is not making cases is a group that will not receive buy money, and since that resource is always thought to be in short supply, there are financial as well as status reasons for making cases.

Many thoughtful agents dislike the time they devote to Class III violators; all agents would prefer to arrest Class I violators. Frustrated by their inability to make big cases, they blame it on the system—what they claim to be the pressure for stats from their supervisors (which the supervisors deny) or what they feel is the public relations or political necessity of making stats (which the congressional committees with jurisdiction in these matters have explicitly disavowed).

The management task force, while aware of the problem, was unwilling to abandon G-DEP entirely: it was necessary for purposes of "program analysis" and "to assist in evaluating DEA's overall mission accomplishments."[18] But G-DEP should not be used, it argued, "for comparing regional accomplishments, for allocating resources to the Field, or for rating regions."[19] Such views are not likely to have any effect on the regions or the agents; the mere *existence* of the numbers and the absence of conspicuous evidence of rewards flowing to persons who do poorly on G-DEP statistics but well in other, equally visible ways, will leave agents and RDs skeptical that anything has changed.

Not only has the G-DEP system not achieved its goal of showing that resources are focussed on high-level violators, it has not been an effective tool for directing resources toward particular drugs. When John Bartels and later Henry Dogin were DEA administrators, they sought to increase enforcement efforts devoted to dangerous drugs (amphetamines, barbiturates, and the like). Most operators in the organization were aware of the emphasis, but relatively little happened as a result. In the first six months of 1974, arrests of dangerous-drug traffickers by the DEA alone in its domestic regions totalled 644, less than 20 percent of all DEA arrests.[20] A year and a half later, during the last six months of 1975, dangerous-drug arrests by the DEA acting alone were less than 15 percent of the total (in that period, heroin accounted for 41 percent and cocaine for 26.4 percent of the arrests).[21] As one administrator of a DEA region explained it, "Formally, dangerous drugs are important—Bartels said so. Informally, agents believe that heroin and cocaine are more important, and to change that you would have to brainwash them or reward and pressure them."

The agents' perceptions tended to support their heroin orientation. The agency, and (with one exception) its predecessors, had a long tradition of "fighting heroin." The exception, the old Bureau of Drug Abuse Control in HEW, provided the DEA with some of the few agents who attach importance to dangerous drugs. In most regional offices, relatively few enforcement groups were given special responsibility for dangerous drugs—only four out of the twenty-five in the New York Regional Office, for example. Agents believe that in the competition for scarce buy money, having a heroin case is an advantage. Penalties given by judges to dangerous-drug violators are much less, on the average, than those given to heroin traffickers. During fiscal 1975, about the same proportion (roughly three fourths) of those charged with narcotics and dangerous-drug trafficking were convicted in federal district courts, but whereas two thirds of those convicted on narcotics charges went to prison, only one half of those convicted on "controlled substances" charges were imprisoned.[22] Many agents interpret this to mean that judges and the public generally think of dangerous drugs as "kiddie dope" that is not to be taken seriously. The chances, under these circumstances, of flipping a defendant into an informant are, in the opinion of agents, small. Against these pressures, administrative admonitions have little weight.

The interest in heroin and cocaine is not all-consuming,

however, for two reasons, one psychological and the other structural. Agents derive their greatest satisfaction from arresting big and obviously wicked dealers—persons who are rich, clever, especially corrupt, and notably successful in their illicit trade. To an agent, a major marijuana or LSD dealer can be as big and therefore as bad as a major heroin dealer. The agent's task on the street is essentially a test of wits against an elusive and wary adversary. The trafficker is not a statistic or even a legal classification, but an opponent. Few agents would ignore a big marijuana dealer in favor of a lesser heroin dealer, whatever their feelings about the nature of the drugs. This attitude probably could not be altered by management, even if it should want to.

The structural reason could be changed, but for political reasons to be explained in chapters 6 and 7, is not likely to be. Many agents are assigned to offices located in states with no significant heroin problem, or at least with few or no chances for finding a Class I heroin dealer. At one time, the G-DEP system did not provide for a Class I marijuana dealer. This meant that some agents and some field offices, owing to their location, could never make a Class I arrest. Protests from the field led headquarters to revise the system so that the largest marijuana dealers would fall into Class I. In a decentralized organization, equity requires that every unit have a chance at the big prize.

Administrators and Operators

In neither the FBI nor the DEA do operators—agents—perceive administrators above their first-line supervisors as especially helpful. This is particularly true of headquarters administrators nominally involved in case supervision or agent evaluation. The FBI has gathered opinion data that supports this generalization; a comparable survey in the DEA would, I believe, produce similar results. The FBI survey, carried out in February 1974, found that most agents had a favorable attitude toward their immediate superiors but a negative attitude toward headquarters. Group supervisors expressed confidence in FBI personnel but disliked the amount of supervision they received from headquarters.[23]

In any complex organization, operators are likely to take a dim view of the knowledge and behavior of "the brass." Routine griping about burdensome policies and unsympathetic officials is commonplace in any setting. Many of the procedures about which personnel may complain are absolutely necessary, however annoying—it is essential to investigate integrity problems, maintain financial accountability, and ensure that communications and files are accurate and complete. No doubt most operators would prefer to be left entirely alone to do the job as they see fit, whatever the consequences for equity and efficiency.

The administrative systems of the FBI and the DEA are not problems simply because agents complain of them, however, but because they have not been rationally related to the critical tasks that the operators perform. FBI agents, or at least those assigned to criminal work, receive and investigate complaints alleging violations of federal statutes; in so doing, they interview citizens and develop informants. To judge their work, collectively and individually, one would want to know how many complaints they receive, what proportion are solved and what proportion closed for other reasons (an unfounded complaint or an absence of leads), and what characteristics of the cases are more or less likely to lead to solutions. To guide them in the allocation of their scarce time and resources, one would want to make distinctions among cases and leads from other offices in terms of their seriousness and importance and develop guidelines to help assess the prosecutive potential of cases.

The Bureau's administrative system does not count complaints, does not (except for bank robberies) calculate solution rates, does not assess the reasons for closing a case or the characteristics of cases that are more or less vulnerable to investigation, does not (except at the extremes) distinguish among cases by any measure of seriousness, and insists that all leads from other offices be followed whether significant or trivial. The development of informants has not been monitored closely except (until recently) for statistical purposes. Cases are not reviewed to see if all opportunities to develop informants were exploited. Instead, the administrative system counts "matters pending" (without distinction among kinds of matters), convictions, fines, savings, and recoveries, the last three despite the nearly unanimous view among agents and supervisors interviewed that these numbers are of little significance. Apart from this, the administrative processes of the Bureau have been designed, not to supervise rationally the performance of an agent's central tasks, but to ensure compliance with rules specifying standards for managing paperwork and records and for the use of money, equipment, and manpower. These processes are means oriented, intended to ensure uniformity in the use of inputs, and not goal oriented. Indeed, scarcely anyone in the Bureau speaks of "goals."

The DEA would seem to differ. Its reporting system is based on an elaborate classification of arrests and seizures so as to induce the production of "quality" arrests and major cases. But the very effort to achieve this has, paradoxically, produced an even greater emphasis on quantity—large numbers of Class III and Class IV cases. Moreover, the decentralized structure of the agency combined with the perceived dependence of rewards—advancement, resources, publicity—on making cases has led to a tendency to hoard leads and informants so as to maximize the individual benefits of agents and the territorial advantages of regions. Throughout most of the agency's history, little effort was made to oversee, much less to influence, the development and use of its single most valuable resource—informants. As a result, not only were some agents devoting too much effort to unproductive cases and too little to important ones, but agency administrators were in a weak position to cope with public criticism that the DEA was arresting "too many" minor traffickers.

A reader encountering these facts for the first time might suppose that they are the result of "bureaucracy" generally or of particularly narrow or unenlightened bureaucrats in particular. Whether bureaucratic organization necessarily leads to such outcomes is a matter we shall consider later, but here it should be made absolutely clear that the administrators of both agencies are, on the whole, quite aware of these problems, and they frequently bemoan them. Indeed, much of what I have learned of the two agencies I have learned from their own administrators, most of whom are intelligent and perceptive. The problem is not that narrow-minded bureaucrats allow irrational administrative arrangements to persist, but that these arrangements persist despite the concerns and efforts of well-intentioned officials. Why that should be the case is the central problem to which this study is addressed, and in the next two chapters an attempt will be made to answer it. Before doing so, however, some account must be given of the efforts by administrators to make the supervision of agents more rational and thereby to enhance the organization's ability to perform its central tasks.

CHAPTER

5

Administrative Issues

SCHOLARS and other observers of organizational behavior often suppose that they perceive in bureaucracies problems and irrationalities of which the agency members are unaware or which they attempt to correct by manifestly inappropriate means. Outsiders speak patronizingly of bureaucratic conduct that is (to the citizen) wrong-headed or (to the academic) "dysfunctional." In my experience this condescension is rarely justified. To a degree that may astonish those who suppose that "bureaucracy" is the result of a personal failing akin to alcoholism, individual bureaucrats are quite aware of the problems of their agencies and have thought of all (and tried some) of the cures that outsiders might suggest. The bureaucrats may overvalue the ends the organization is to serve or even (I should say especially) overvalue the organization itself, but within the context of a given set of tasks, they are, on the whole, clear-eyed and reasonable.

The important thing to explain about the FBI and the DEA is not why certain fundamental problems have escaped official notice (they have not) or why no efforts are made to correct these problems (they frequently are), but why the remedies are so difficult to implement and, often, so unproductive of the desired results.

One obvious reason—and certainly among FBI and DEA members, the most frequently cited reason—for the organizations' inability to devise an administrative strategy well suited to the management of their tasks is that the tasks do not lend themselves to management at all. And there is much truth in this. The work of detectives consists essentially of interviewing or manipulating apprehensive persons in intimate settings regarding complex or sensitive matters that do not lend themselves to measurement or even summary statement. Law enforcement does not produce a product that can be weighed on a scale or a service that can be (easily) priced on a market; law enforcement is a set of human relationships—victim-suspect, victim-witness, suspect-investigator, witness-investigator—that is at least as subtle as the relationships between pupil and teacher, patient and doctor, or even friend and friend. Any effort to extract the essential elements of these relationships or their results and convert them into quantitative or otherwise easily understood terms is bound to be in some important degree misleading and may even distort the process that it seeks to measure.

Almost any FBI or DEA agent will, in different but more colorful language, heartily subscribe to this view. A detective wants, above all else, to be left alone and to be backed up. Unfortunately, if he is left entirely alone he cannot count on being backed up (superiors who place no constraints on him may later decide, when conflict arises, that he was wrong). But even among administrators, there is a widespread conviction that any effort at "management by objectives" is a mistake because however great the need for supervision, it cannot be accomplished by setting explicit, substantive objectives and measuring progress toward them. The effort by the Department of Justice in the mid-1970s to install a management-by-objectives budget system was resisted within the FBI and to a lesser degree within the DEA. Though compliance occurred, it was largely *pro forma.* The reason for the difference in response arises out of the difference between the investigative and instigative task. Investigators respond to unpredictable behaviors in their environment by making retrospective inquiries to find out who produced the behavior; instigators can, within limits, produce their own workload by prospectively seeking to induce someone to commit a crime in their presence. For the FBI, management by objectives is meaningless ("how do we know how many kidnappings there will be?"); for the DEA, it is gamesmanship ("they want stats, we'll give 'em stats").

But this general posture does not settle the matter. Administration exists, and if clever ideas may not make things better, current practices can make them worse. The pressure for statistical accomplishments in the FBI was clearly making things hard for the agents by forcing them to divert substantial resources from cases they and their supervisors regarded as important and toward matters that were significant only because somebody counted them. The G-DEP system, a form of management-by-objectives, was not producing as many high-level cases as some wanted and was drawing attention to, without changing, the number of low-level arrests being made. Each organization has tried seriously to cope with these problems.

FBI: Quality over Quantity

In the early 1970s, a Bureau survey[1] indicated that 60 percent of the cases presented for prosecution by FBI agents were being declined by United States attorneys (USAs) not because the quality of the investigation was poor but because either the substantive violation alleged was, in the opinion of the USA, trivial or the prospect of making an arrest of the guilty party was slight. There were two issues. One arose because USAs were tired of having to go through the motions of declining prosecution on cases that the FBI knew could not be prosecuted but that Bureau rules required be presented to the USA. A typical case of this sort would be a theft from a railroad boxcar moving in interstate commerce when no one knew when or where or by whom the boxcar was pilfered. There was no chance of finding a culprit because there was no one worth interviewing. Under FBI rules, however, this was a "pending matter," "all logical leads" had to be followed, and the FBI agent who had the ticket could not close the case on his own authority. Hence, a letter was sent to the USA.

The other issue involved cases in which the FBI might in fact be able to make an arrest but for a charge that the USA did not believe warranted federal prosecution—a minor theft, for example. Many USAs believed that if the FBI stopped making such cases they would be able to initiate more important investigations involving such matters as "white-collar" crime, civil rights violations, political corruption, and frauds against the government. (In this, they may have been mistaken—though the FBI workload will affect to some degree the kinds of cases they bring, I suspect, for reasons to be discussed later, that other factors are more important.)

This criticism of the FBI came after Hoover's death and, even more important, after the creation at FBI headquarters of an Office of Planning and Evaluation reporting directly to the director. This meant that an alternative to the Administrative Division existed in which a highly sensitive operating issue might be considered—highly sensitive because any change in caseload policies might have important effects on the size, staffing, and resources of field offices. Clarence Kelley, who had recently become FBI Director, assigned the issue to the OPE. After much study, the OPE recommended that a six-month experiment be conducted in which four field offices would be allowed to close immediately marginal or weak cases without presenting them to the USA and without keeping them open for statistical purposes. The object was to cut back the caseload so as to free resources for the investigation of more serious cases or for the initiation of new kinds of investigations.

The SACs viewed the change apprehensively. All knew that their statistics on "pending matters" were inflated and misleading, but all also believed that headquarters allocated men and resources to field offices on the basis of these case-loads. Meetings of SACs were held to discuss the change and to reassure them—not always successfully—that the experiment would not lead to their offices losing resources. The SACs in the four experimental field offices agreed to try (they had no choice), but one was obviously reluctant and provided only minimal cooperation and only one of the four was obviously enthusiastic. When the experiment ended in March 1975, there had been a drop of 27 percent in the caseloads of the four field offices, ranging from 19 percent in the office headed by the reluctant SAC to 42 percent in the office headed by the enthusiastic one.

What other changes accompanied the drop in workload was a matter of dispute. The OPE believed elimination of minor cases permitted the field offices to initiate new, more important investigations, to raise (in one case) the bank robbery clearance rate, and to reduce the time it took to cover leads sent in from other offices.[2] Other headquarters administrators and many SACs were not convinced. To some, the policy smacked of "selective law enforcement"—giving attention to some crimes, neglecting the rest—while others were skeptical that anything really changed if you merely weeded out the minor cases that no one was seriously investigating anyhow. An effort to measure the time it took to cover leads before and during the experiment was inconclusive; overall, the time seemed to drop slightly, but it went up for one kind of crime and remained the same for

another. And few SACs were persuaded that the OPE rec-
ommendation to disregard caseloads in allocating manpower
really meant what it said.

Director Kelley was convinced, however, and on August
28, 1975, ordered the "Quality over Quantity" program to
be instituted Bureau-wide. Each SAC was to set priorities as
to the kinds of cases that were important in his area and to
concentrate resources on them. Statistics were to be down-
played. Within a year, the results were being felt. The total
number of pending cases declined by 23 percent and the
average caseload per agent fell from 26.1 to 19.1.[3] The
number of convictions from some crimes (bank robbery,
bank fraud, government fraud, and interstate transportation
of stolen property) went up despite the decline in the
number of investigative matters pending while the number
of convictions for other offenses (motor vehicle theft, copyright violations, and theft of government property) went
down, but by less than the decrease in the number of pending matters. Overall, the ratio of convictions to pending matters increased.

The changes in some crime categories were huge. In one
field office, in the space of eighteen months (July 1974 to
December 1975), the number of pending auto-theft cases
declined from 624 to 158, a drop of 75 percent. In the same
office during the same period, pending bank robbery cases
fell by 54 percent, thefts from interstate shipment by 55 percent, and thefts of government property by 53 percent.
There was no immediate decline in the number of prosecutions or any significant decline in the number of convictions.

The agents were on the whole pleased with the change.
As one experienced supervisor put it, the Bureau "eliminated the charades." The pressure on agents to keep up a
certain caseload for statistical purposes was lessened and accordingly the paperwork and diversion of energy necessary
to process "junk" cases became smaller.

The crimes for which the sharpest changes occurred were,

of course, those most likely to involve small losses or un-known subjects: primarily, thefts. When an out-of-state stolen automobile is recovered by a local police department, the Bureau no longer adds the vehicle to its caseload unless it appears to be the work of a criminal "ring" or unless there is a known subject who is a serious repeater. Minor thefts from interstate shipments or from government buildings are closed summarily. The crimes in which little decline in case-load occurred were those that, by definition, almost cer-tainly involved major losses (interstate shipment of stolen property valued at $5,000 or more), a major threat to per-sonal safety (kidnapping), or a known subject (unauthorized flight to avoid prosecution). The decline in bank robbery cases was more puzzling: surely bank robbery is a serious of-fense, usually involving sizable money losses and often pos-ing a threat to the life of the victims. In fact, the bank rob-bery case file in several field offices had regularly been padded by opening cases on individual bank robbery *sus-pects* as well as crimes in order to keep the "stats" of the bank robbery squad high. With the new policy, individual suspect files were dropped.

While it is clear that major changes occurred in the number of trivial or unproductive matters that cluttered the caseloads of agents and USAs, it is far from clear that there was any Bureau-wide redirection of effort in setting priori-ties for or allocating resources to the investigation of impor-tant cases. In the field office studied most closely, agents continued to work the same kinds of cases in the same ways, though now free of the burdens of maintaining in an active status large numbers of "junk" cases. There were no in-creases in cases involving bankruptcy, loansharking, or fraud against the government, and there were declines in the number of bank fraud and copyright cases. The "Quality over Quantity" program did not prove to be a strategy to improve the management of significant cases, but only a means to remove impediments to such management. Nowhere was this more evident than in the area of "white-collar" crime.

FBI: "White-Collar" Crime

The director of the FBI and the attorney general of the United States joined with many others during 1975–76 in calling for more intensive enforcement of the laws against "white-collar" crime. I put this term in quotation marks because it has no legal meaning and only an ambiguous popular one. To some, it means any crime committed by an upper-status person—a businessman, government official, doctor, lawyer, or whatever—but that is not a particularly useful distinction. A doctor who murders his wife has not done anything that is legally or behaviorally different from a day laborer who murders *his* wife. To others, the phrase refers to crimes committed by persons who have privileged access to opportunities for significant illicit gains: a bank teller in a position to embezzle funds, a corporate president able to convert company assets to his own use or to evade income taxes, or a government official with the power to extract bribes from persons seeking his favor. But while these behaviors are all crimes, there is no reason to consider them as a single category. A person taking a bribe is doing something quite different from a person who dips into the cash drawer—in the former case, there is a co-conspirator but no obvious victim, while in the latter case there is an obvious and unwitting victim. To still others, "white-collar" crime is a label meant to draw attention to the activities of persons who break laws, not entirely or perhaps even primarily for their own gain, but on behalf of large organizations, especially corporations: the businessman who rigs prices by conspiring with a competitor or who obtains lucrative contracts by bribing public officials.

There is no way to choose among these possible meanings of the term except by asking what purpose the definition is to serve and then attempting to devise a definition that draws together a single, more-or-less homogeneous set of behaviors that is interesting given that purpose. For the purposes of this study, what is important is the way in which the nature of the crime affects the task of law enforcement agencies. From that perspective, the status and motives of a lawbreaker are of less significance for investigators than the kind of *victimization* produced. Though one can easily imagine ways in which status and motives might affect law enforcement (some detectives might fear the political or social consequences of investigating the rich or powerful, others might be more or less tolerant of certain behaviors depending on the motives of the actors), and though one should always look carefully for evidence that status or motives are improperly influencing law enforcement, one must still ask how investigators can attack a problem even assuming they are free from inappropriate influences. The argument of chapter 2 is that, essentially, the way in which victims are produced chiefly shapes the law enforcement task, and that this is the case because law enforcement agencies overwhelmingly rely on victim/witness cooperation to solve crimes and make arrests. In those cases in which the crime does not produce an obvious victim, as with drug trafficking, the detectives must themselves become witnesses to the illegal acts by adopting the role of instigator.

Crimes loosely referred to as "white collar" can be sorted into more useful categories by asking whether, or to what extent, the crime produces an unwitting, self-conscious, cooperative victim who experiences a significant loss. Obviously, bank robbery and hijacking produce victims that are innocent and immediately aware of suffering a significant loss. From a law enforcement point of view, such crimes are no different from burglary, auto theft, or other "street" crimes. But they are also no different from embezzlement or passing bad checks, crimes that are sometimes thought of as "white collar." These crimes will be termed *predatory*.

At the other extreme are *consensual* crimes, such as drug trafficking, gambling, and prostitution. (Whether such crimes are also "victimless" is another and more complicated question. Chronic heroin abuse certainly produces, by most standards, a victim; the difference is that the "victim" has more or less freely consented to some of the transactions that produced the drug dependency.) Consensual crimes also include some instances of bribery (where the giving and receiving of the bribe is entirely voluntary and no obvious victim results) and what is sometimes called "honest graft" in which, for example, a government official rewards a party stalwart with a lucratic contract in violation of competitive bidding laws but at a price that is not substantially different from the competitive price. It also includes loansharking, at least insofar as violence is not employed.

Between the predatory and the consensual are at least two other kinds of crime. One is *extortionate*. By this I mean those crimes that produce a clear victim who suffers a significant loss, but who is disinclined to cooperate with law enforcement officers because he or she fears reprisals from the offender. This includes many kinds of assaults, especially among acquaintances, blackmail, loansharking accompanied by violence or the threat of violence, and kidnappings in which the victim's relatives fear greatly for his or her safety.

Finally, and closest perhaps to the core of many popular conceptions of "white-collar" crime, are those cases in which a victim is produced, but the victim is either unaware of the loss or perceives the loss to be below his threshold of complaint. These are *collective* victimizations, the total illicit gains may be quite large but *per victim* they are low or invisible. Such crimes include tax evasion, smuggling, much price fixing, misuse of corporate or union funds, political corruption ("dishonest graft"), and many forms of consumer deception, professional malpractice, and illegal environmental degradation. Lest one suppose that these offenses are always the product of corporate or professional misconduct, recall that the firm may also be the victim, not only of other firms that act unfairly in the market, but of customers and employees who steal merchandise.

To the FBI, as to most law enforcement agencies, those so-called white-collar crimes that are predatory in nature present no problems other than those resulting from scarce investigative resources. Most bank frauds handled by the FBI are of this sort. An employee, often a teller or an officer, steals money from the bank. The shortages are revealed by an audit. A suspect is easily identified. Though the case may become extremely complex if the embezzler covered his tracks skillfully, the investigation is entirely consistent with the traditional definition of the FBI task and with the experience of the agent. Since accounting procedures are complex, most field offices have an "accounting squad" composed of agents with specialized training to handle such cases. In one field office, about 100 fraud cases were handled a year and in another, about 200. These numbers did not change much in response to the "Quality" program. A large field office may obtain 50 or 60 convictions a year in this area. It is rarely necessary to develop informants, as suspect and victims are easily identified and known to each other.

Consensual crimes depend entirely on the development of informants or on the surreptitious collection of evidence by means of wiretaps and electronic surveillance. While it is easy to understand why this might be so with respect to gambling or narcotics, it is important to bear in mind that such methods are also necessary with the more consensual forms of "white-collar" crimes as well. Bribery cases involve informants, plea bargaining, and offers of immunity. (Those observers who find such methods objectionable when employed in narcotics cases should pause before erecting their

objection into a principle and reflect on whether they wish
to bar the use of these methods in investigating corporate or
governmental consensual crimes.) Skill at developing such
cases is rare, and in most offices only a few agents have the
ability and perseverance (and freedom from administrative
constraints) to follow up on tips, persuade reluctant participants to cooperate with the Bureau, and build a prosecut-
able case.

Because of the investigative difficulties or the rarity of the
event or some combination of both, bribery cases are relatively infrequent. One large field office had between 5 and
10 such matters pending at any given time (the office had responsibility for several states); another, located in a state
reputed to be among the more corrupt, also had about 10.
Only a tiny number of prosecutions result.

Between these two extremes are the extortionate and collective crimes. In the former case, the problem is to persuade a fearful victim to testify; in the latter, it is to learn that
any victimization has occurred at all. In the language of
police analysts, such investigations are highly "proactive"—
the investigator must find and cultivate leads rather than
react to cases that are brought by victims.

The traditional organization of an FBI field office does not
lend itself to proactive investigations. Squads are organized
around workloads, which means that the high-volume cases
become the concern of a squad specializing in those matters.
But squad organization based on volume means a field office
structure determined by victim complaints. Accordingly, almost every field office has a squad devoted to auto theft,
another to thefts from interstate shipments, another to "accounting matters" (i.e., bank frauds), and so on. There are,
of course, major exceptions to this: one or more squads will
be devoted to security matters and (usually) one to organized
crime.

Giving priority to consensual, collective, or extortionate
crime means reorganizing a field office around a proactive

rather than reactive investigative strategy. But no office can adopt such a strategy completely, for to do so would leave no one to answer the hundreds, even thousands, of victim complaints regarding predatory crime that arrive each year. Obviously, some balance must be struck. Finding that balance, however, is a risky enterprise, for the FBI's reputation—a reputation that constitutes a valuable investigative asset—was chiefly made by the quick, sometimes dramatic, solution of predatory crimes—bank robberies, kidnappings, and major thefts. To commit the organization to a new direction is not without its risks.

Beginning with Philadelphia, several of the larger field offices have begun to reorganize so as to give proactive investigations greater priority. The experiences of one of these illustrates what is involved and at stake. In December 1975, the SAC adopted a proactive or "target" approach. Twenty-two agents were assigned to two "general crime" squads charged with responding to victim complaints regarding the traditional crime classifications—theft, robbery, kidnapping, bad checks, and fugitives. The remaining ninety-one agents doing criminal work were assigned to eight "target" squads concerned with consensual, extortionate, and dispersed crimes. The assignment of each target squad was not based chiefly on types of crime but on types of offenders—businessmen, local government officials, labor leaders, the business affairs of the federal government, and organized crime groups. Each squad was instructed to search out cases involving such persons by cultivating informants and pursuing leads from other government agencies as well as by responding to citizen and victim complaints. Each was to employ whatever federal laws seemed appropriate in building a case rather than being confined to a single crime category. The reorganization involved a massive shift of resources; more than seventy agents who once were doing reactive or security work were put into proactive work. As a supervisor later explained to an interviewer, "The SAC said, 'get rid of the crap and work the big cases.'"

The target cases are developed in part out of victim complaints by transferring those matters that seemed to involve large criminal organizations or "white-collar" participants from the general crime squads to a target squad and in part by developing tips from friendly reporters, exploring leads from grand jury investigations, interviewing disgruntled businessmen and labor leaders about their competitors, following up on complaints from lawyers and creditors in bankruptcy cases, and staying in touch with federal regulatory agencies to learn of instances of noncompliance that might represent criminal violations.

To develop such cases, a squad must work closely with a cooperative assistant United States attorney (AUSA). While an agent can interview suspects and citizens, it must be "on the record"; the AUSA can talk to such persons informally. An agent can conduct a surveillance, but only an AUSA can offer immunity or subpoena people and records. Agents may develop informants, but to bargain with a prospective informant facing criminal charges the consent of the AUSA is necessary. What kinds of offenders a target squad will be most effective in investigating will depend, therefore, on the priorities and interests of the local USA office, and that in turn is in large part a matter of chance and personality. In this field office, for example, labor corruption cases have become only recently a prime investigative target, in part because before 1975 there was no FBI squad specializing in them and in part because of late one AUSA has become, in one agent's words, "gung ho on labor prosecutions." Once investigative energy is displayed and some prosecutions result, there is an increase in the amount of information volunteered by citizens that can contribute to additional investigations. One group supervisor described the process this way:

> Union guys sneak in and tell us, sometimes because they've lost an election. . . . We get cases referred from the Department of Labor. . . . The only problem is, we can get the reputation of being union busters, so we have to try to spread the indictments around so we get various crafts, different political parties, and so on.

Not all the target cases are of offenders who wear white collars. Many involve those active in predatory crime but on a large or organized scale—hijacking rings, major fences of stolen property, and burglars and jewel thieves operating interstate. These cases are familiar to all FBI agents and for some years there has been a Bureau-wide "Top Thief" program designed to identify and arrest such suspects. In this field office, however, more manpower is committed to a squad with that special mission.

Substantial prosecutions resulted. In a little over a year, township supervisors, state legislators, judges, state tax officials, and school board members were convicted for various corrupt acts, including smuggling, extortion, and bribery. In addition, labor leaders were convicted for illegal union practices and businessmen and bankers for illegal acts in real estate and mortgage financing.

These cases, all heavily publicized, are clearly important, but statistically they count for no more than the conviction of a man stealing a typewriter from a veterans' hospital. Overall, this office experienced during the first six months of its "target" program a 21 percent decline in the number of pending matters and a 25 percent decline in the number of convictions. The SAC, before he began this program, had to convince himself that his personnel, resources, and status would not suffer in consequence of these numerical changes. Obviously, this SAC was convinced, but he is, in the words of almost everyone who speaks of him, "a maverick." Few other SACs followed his example at the time. The threatening implications of such statistics can be meliorated by sympathetic executive leadership at FBI headquarters, and that leadership (not without opposition) has been exercised. Director Kelley conspicuously increased the manpower of the innovative field office despite the smaller caseload. This action reassured several other apprehensive SACs, at least for the time being. In the long run however, the apprehension about change will remain since, obviously, not every office with a smaller caseload can have its manpower increased.

A problem of greater immediate importance is that of having, in the words of one agent, "an A team and a B team" in the field office. The "A team" works on the target squads and handles the big, publicity-laden cases; the "B team" works on the general crime squads and handles, in the words of another agent, "the garbage." For one of the general crime squads, this status problem is less severe because it is assigned predatory crimes that require an immediate response—bank robberies, kidnappings, airplane hijackings, and bombings. These are often important, even dramatic events, and no one need feel himself a second-class agent because he is involved in one. Important as these matters continue to be, however, the assignment to a general crime squad of this sort implies a substantial reallocation of status within the office. Once, the bank robbery squad was the elite FBI unit—"fast cars and big cigars," in the old Bureau adage—but now in this office the target squads, which with few exceptions do not touch bank robberies, are the elite units. The change in status is made vivid by the personnel assignment polices—the general crime squads get the youngest agents, the target squads get the more experienced ones.

The other general crime squad has the high-volume cases—thefts, fugitives, crimes on government property, bad checks, and the like. The eleven agents on the squad had, in mid-1976, nearly 1,000 pending criminal matters. As the supervisor said, "It's too much work to manage. It's that simple. It takes all day just to handle the paper." This workload, combined with the relaxation of the pressure to maintain high loads for statistical purposes, has meant that the operating ethos of this squad has become one of closing out cases as quickly as possible. Drastic reductions in the effective workload are obtained by refusing to consider most auto-theft cases and by minimizing the attention given fugitives, especially if they are deserters from the armed forces. Small thefts from interstate commerce are ignored. The incentives to explore victim complaints to see if they hold the promise of developing into a major criminal prosecution are weakened, not only by the sheer force of numbers, but also by the realization that should a promising major investigation emerge it might well be reassigned to a target squad and then, as the supervisor explained, "the agent's morale goes to hell." Furthermore, the very effort to create target squads implies that some crimes are more important than others; few agents are inclined to work hard on matters their superiors have declared in advance to be unimportant.

Some of these problems can be handled by additional resources. With more agents working general predatory crime, the pressure to close out matters will be lessened. But no marginal change in resources will alter the ethos of an office based, as it is, on rather clear perceptions of the way in which status is distributed. The target squad concept may well prove in the long run the best approach, given a certain level of resources. It certainly has represented the greatest administrative change at the operator level that has occurred in an FBI office in many years. The program is properly controversial only insofar as there is controversy over whether the objects of the target squads—organized, dispersed, and consensual crime—ought to receive greater efforts than predatory crime. Factually, it is too soon to judge the impact of the lessened attention to victim-initiated complaints. From one perspective, such matters ought to be chiefly the province of local police departments that share jurisdiction with the FBI over these crimes. But from another, such matters might get no investigation at all if not from the FBI. Furthermore, servicing victim complaints is important for more reasons than simply the desirability of solving a crime, especially since the chances of solving most such crimes are quite low. Victims and citizens are valuable sources of information, and as one supervisor remarked, "when we don't take cases, people don't call us."

FBI: Program Management

The "Quality" case program and the emphasis on "white-collar" crime were only part of a more general shift in administrative philosophy in FBI headquarters stimulated by Clarence Kelley. To him, what the Bureau and its admirers had long described as among its great strengths—centralized control over all phases of operations—was in fact its great weakness. It had led, in his eyes, to an emphasis on statistical accomplishments, case-by-case review through an elaborate tickler system (described in chapter 4), and a top-heavy headquarters staff. The informational system of the Bureau was organized around individual cases and individual crime categories, making it difficult if not impossible to consider in a systematic way the allocation of resources among kinds of crimes, the relative importance of different cases, and the manpower needs of field offices. Furthermore, the emphasis on the specific crime category impeded the effort, pioneered in the field office described in the preceding section, to direct resources against certain kinds of offenders (racketeers, corrupt businessmen and politicians) who might, in a given instance, be found violating any one of a dozen different statutes. The "program management" concept was designed to facilitate the adoption by the entire field of the "targeting" strategy.

In addition, program management was the Bureau's way of responding to the demand by the Department of Justice that it adopt a "management-by-objectives" system. In the face of widespread skepticism in the Bureau, certain key headquarters personnel, especially in the Office of Planning and Evaluation, were determined to find a way of allocating resources toward priority cases, reducing agent attention to lesser but high-volume victim-initiated cases, and measuring in a more meaningful way progress toward investigative objectives.

Three important changes were made. First, a new statistical reporting system was designed that would emphasize the results of investigations in prosecutorial rather than financial terms. For the first time, each field office was to report the number of cases closed by the SAC or declined for prosecution by the United States attorney as well as those cases resulting in complaints issued by a USA or indictments handed down by a federal grand jury. A study by the General Accounting Office had revealed that during a four-month period in 1976 only about 9 percent of the cases studied in six field offices were accepted for prosecution; half the cases had been closed administratively by the SAC and over 40 percent had been declined by the USA.[4] Now such information would be regularly available to Bureau officials. In addition, no further effort was to be made to count "savings" as an accomplishment. Finally, the results of prosecution were to be measured more precisely: only one conviction per person convicted was to count (instead, as previously, of counting as a "conviction" each separate count of an indictment or each indictment against a single individual who was found guilty) and the sentence received was to be recorded for each person convicted.

Second, the Investigative Division was reorganized as described in chapter 4 in order to bring together similar cases in one supervisory section, to emphasize organized and "white-collar" crime, and to eliminate the tickler system of individual case supervision. That system had served well the organizational interests of J. Edgar Hoover: rarely did anyone in headquarters have to tell his boss that he was not familiar with a particular case or that he did not know whether the agent in the field was up-to-date in filing his paperwork on it. But this form of supervision served no substantial investigative purpose, though it did supply headquarters with ample ammunition to use against the field for disciplinary purposes, should the need arise. Under the new plan, the ninety-day status reports on cases were to be phased out and

replaced with a "prosecutive report" filed with headquarters
and the local United States attorney when the investigation
was substantially complete and ready for prosecution. When
implemented, headquarters supervisors would learn nothing about cases except for administrative matters (for example, requests for authorization to use body recorders or
install wiretaps) until the investigation was complete, and
they would be under instructions to supervise the field by
examining, not individual cases, but statistical records and
groups of cases.

Third, a new method was to be devised for allocating
resources, especially personnel, among field offices. The old
system was simplicity itself. The total caseload of each field
office was divided by what was thought to be the appropriate
caseload per agent (roughly, 30 cases) and the result was the
number of agents each office should have. The perverse incentives this created for SACs are not hard to imagine. To
maintain or enhance the resources available to them, SACs
would strive to increase the caseload of each agent by insisting that a separate "case" be opened on every matter, however trivial, and that when necessary new cases be found by,
for example, canvassing local police departments to find stolen cars that had been recovered from interstate commerce
so that a federal "car case" could be claimed. As one headquarters official later remarked, "the Hoover system was
logically indefensible but it worked" because allocation decisions could be routinized and justified. Political maneuver-
ing to get more resources was minimized. You either had
the caseload or you did not. Indeed, so strong was (and is)
the concern of SACs over resource questions that when
Director Kelley began the "Quality over Quantity" experiment he had to promise the SACs that no reductions in personnel in any field office would be made as a result of declining workloads for "six months to a year."

The problem is not to criticize the old formula but to find
a better one that will both serve the objectives of program

management and minimize administrative strain and stress. It is not clear that any such formula can be found. The Office of Planning and Evaluation has been struggling with the problem, but thus far to no avail. Its best effort to date (mid-1977) has been to produce an elaborate checklist of criteria to be taken into account, grouped into "static factors" (such as population, geographic area, urbanization, industrial development, the presence of state capitals and other government facilities) and "dynamic factors" (such as the existence of organized crime or political corruption, the level of espionage and terrorist activity, and the general crime level). The "static factors" are to be used to determine the minimum necessary level of manpower, the "dynamic factors" to justify additional increments of manpower to serve high-priority investigative objectives.

The field offices are skeptical, and headquarters knows it. To the former, program management is a good idea in general but a threat in practice. SACs fear losing personnel and complain of "selective law enforcement." Privately, OPE members admit that if the new allocation system were perfected and implemented, there would be an "overwhelming change in the size of field offices—the rural and small-town areas would lose manpower and the major urban areas would gain." But the OPE knows this is politically unacceptable and thus, "We're not going to do it." Furthermore, once one abandons the old caseload method, there literally is *no* nonarbitrary method for calculating the "correct" resource level. When more than one factor is taken into account, those factors must be weighted, and Bureau members will disagree strongly as to what the weights should be. "We can't reduce it to an algebraic formula," one assistant director told an interviewer. "You have to be subjective."

But a subjective method is a controversial one, especially so when the new methods are part of a general plan to deemphasize the role and power of headquarters. At a time when the DEA is under heavy criticism for being too decentralized and needing greater headquarters control, the FBI is moving in precisely the opposite direction. The power of headquarters, and especially of the old Administrative Division, weighed with such a heavy hand on the Bureau that the younger supervisors who are enthusiastic supporters of Director Kelley's new management methods are in part motivated by a desire simply to reduce the influence of Washington in the field. "Sometimes," one said to an interviewer, "I wish this place [headquarters] would dry up and blow away." The problem is that the demands of official Washington and of public pressures on the Bureau may not, for reasons to be discussed in chapter 6, permit any real diminution of headquarters power and that the field, though it resents Washington supervision, fears even more the reallocation of resources and power that may accompany any effort to alter that supervision.

DEA: Interregional Cases

A pervasive and continuing criticism of the DEA has been its alleged inability or unwillingness to emphasize investigations of major drug-trafficking organizations that operate on an interregional or national basis. A subcommittee of the Committee on Government Operations of the United States Senate, in a 1976 report, attacked "indiscriminate undercover techniques and 'buy-bust' tactics" directed at "low-level dealers and addicts" and urged instead that the agency place "heavy emphasis on conspiracy cases in which high-level narcotics traffickers are targeted."[5] The subcommittee did not say how these conspiracy prosecutions were to be obtained.

Even within the DEA, there have been outspoken critics of allowing agents to make so many Class III cases. A former head of the Domestic Investigations Division, who had previously been an agent in the Federal Bureau of Narcotics, compared the DEA unfavorably with the FBN:

> Making the big case—finding the source—was the FBN ethic. Now that's wiped out. In DEA, we've grown rapidly, and the Peter Principle applies. And we've become decentralized, resulting in our activities being focussed on local jurisdictions. We do the easy thing—make a buy.

Later, testifying before the Senate subcommittee, he urged the development of "significant conspiracy cases" and attacked the claims of the administrator of the agency that there had been genuine gains in the proportion of Class I and II violators being arrested.[6]

An outsider reading and hearing these charges might suppose that DEA administrators were opposed to the concept of high-level investigations or favored "buy-bust" arrests. Quite the opposite is the case. Every administrator of the DEA and its predecessor agencies has, without exception, endorsed efforts to make major conspiracy cases, and very few, if any, middle-level managers in the agency can be found who dissent from this goal. And efforts have been made to devote organizational resources specifically to the goal. Yet little seems to change.

The most conspicuous effort to make conspiracy cases has involved the creation of "central tactical units" (CENTACs) operating out of headquarters designed to handle major cases that cut across regional lines. By mid-1976, about a dozen CENTACs had been in operation, each consisting of a group of agents and a supervisor detached from duty in their own regions and reporting directly to headquarters. Each CENTAC would be aimed at a particular illegal organization or trafficking network. One was directed against Lebanese dealers operating in several parts of the world, another at black traffickers in several eastern cities, still another at

Chinese dealers on the West Coast. One of these earlier efforts resulted in eight grand juries producing about 100 indictments against distributors of a dangerous drug.

The early CENTACs were initiated by headquarters, but complaints from regional directors contributed to a change in strategy. The RDs saw a CENTAC as a drain on their resources and opportunities—valuable agents would be taken away, often without warning, and credit for cases begun in one region would be given to another or to a headquarters unit. Many times the agents lost on temporary assignment to a CENTAC would have attributes in short supply in the agency—black agents, for example, or Spanish-speaking ones—so that their reassignment meant reduced opportunities to make cases requiring the use of agents with those traits. The change allowed a region to run or at least to initiate a CENTAC. But other regions were reluctant to cooperate with a region that had a leadership role in a CENTAC, and some of these investigations floundered.

Opinion within the DEA was deeply divided over the CENTAC approach. Some regional directors saw no reason why they could not make all the high-level cases that were necessary, provided that they had sufficient resources, and thus opposed the CENTAC concept entirely. Others favored CENTACs, but only when they were done in cooperation rather than in competition with other regions. Some top administrators favored headquarters-run CENTACs, but even in headquarters, opinion was by no means unanimous. One senior official felt that the "CENTAC concept is OK, but the method is subversive—they tried to force it down the RDs' throats." Another headquarters administrator felt that "CENTACs are bad if they are run by headquarters," and in any event he doubted they produced better arrests than good regional cases.

Developing high-level conspiracy cases appears much more difficult to persons inside the DEA than to those outside. For one thing, the nature of the drug market has changed. When much of the East Coast was supplied with white heroin manufactured in illicit French laboratories from opium produced in Turkey, attacking a few trafficking systems could, and did, make an appreciable difference in the flow of heroin. The so-called "French Connection" was one such case. After the French police, in cooperation with the Americans, seized some laboratories and major drug consignments and the Turkish government eliminated the opium poppy crops, a shortage of heroin was felt on the East Coast beginning in 1972. The street price of the drug rose sharply, its purity declined, and the number of users (as measured by tests administered to arrested persons) dropped. It was this short-run success that led President Richard Nixon to declare, prematurely, that the nation had "turned the corner" in its campaign against drugs. But the void was soon filled. Brown heroin from Mexico, long the major source for the West Coast, slowly spread throughout the country and eventually took over almost the entire market. The street price per pure milligram of heroin declined and heroin use rose.[7]

The Mexican heroin was in some cases imported by large, well-financed organizations, but in many others the suppliers were small operators handling modest quantities. Mexican heroin was distributed in a free enterprise market rather than the oligopolistic one characteristic of French-Turkish white heroin. As a result, there were fewer important conspiracies against which to direct investigation.

In addition, cocaine use spread rapidly. Cocaine differs significantly from heroin in its effects and the kinds of users it attracts—it is a stimulant rather than a narcotic, it does not produce physiological dependence (though it may have other harmful effects), and it is preferred by consumers (at first, musicians, artists, and publicists) more affluent than the typical heroin addict. But though the users differed, the suppliers in many cases did not. The records of local DEA offices suggest that many dealers handled both heroin and cocaine depending on the preferences of the customer and the availability of supplies. The effort to make major conspiracy cases was partially undercut by the order, in 1976, to avoid cocaine cases. In many instances, the development of a case against a large importing organization required that a "coke" case be made, and if coke was to be subordinated, big cases became fewer.

But the most important constraints on making inter-regional cases were the regions and their needs. Critics of the regional directors term them "parochial" and "feudal," implying that the RDs have no interest in the larger goals of the organization. That is too simple a judgment. The RDs believe deeply in the agency's mission, so deeply, indeed, that they are preoccupied by the shortage of those resources they feel are necessary if they are to serve that mission. Buy money is never abundant and good agents are scarce. CEN-TACs threatened RD access to these limited resources, imposed heavier burdens on their offices, and reduced their autonomy in managing such resources as they had.

Intensifying this problem was the shift in the location of the drug-importing systems. Once, New York City was the heroin capital of the world. Today, it still has more addicts and dealers than any other city, perhaps even more in proportion to its population, but the supply systems and key importers are often located elsewhere—Tucson, Los Angeles, Kansas City, Chicago, Detroit. The decentralization of the heroin business that accompanied the national shift to Mexican heroin cost New York its preeminence as a distribution center. To make a good conspiracy case in New York now requires, in many instances, working outside that region. But there are still many large dealers in New York that DEA agents are eager to arrest. Thus, to shift enforcement resources out of New York to other places (as has in fact happened) means to tell New York agents and administrators that they will be able to make even fewer cases than they once did despite the existence of cases to be made.

Finally, the agent himself works, as suggested in a preceding chapter, in a group in which status goes to those who make cases. As one administrator said, they learn to be door-kickers and come to feel that "there is something wrong with a guy who will pass up the buy tonight." Working a CEN-TAC, or any conspiracy case, involves fewer chances to kick in doors. Months of patient, tedious work are required—checking motel registrations, long-distance telephone toll slips, and airplane reservations, or sitting for many dull hours eavesdropping on telephone conversations in order to establish that the alleged members of a conspiracy are in fact acting in concert. Finally, when indictments are secured and there is an opportunity to make arrests, scores of agents and local police who never developed the case are often "in on the kill." The training, experience, and peer expectations of a narcotics agent lead him to like big cases in theory but to make small arrests in practice.

The difficulties the DEA faces in attempting to develop cases against major drug traffickers are not made easier by the way in which federal prosecutors are organized. Local United States attorneys may be as concerned about keeping cases under their control as are RDs. USAs are subject to even less central direction than RDs, and friction between the DEA and USAs is not uncommon.

A DEA administrative system that could alter the investigative process in ways that would concentrate DEA resources on major, organized violators would be very much different from the system now in effect or any that have been proposed by persons in or out of the agency. Furthermore, that administrative system would have to be supported by relations with other investigative agencies and local police departments of the sort that, for political and constitutional reasons, are unlikely to emerge.

Agents would have to be trained and given rewarding work experiences in the paper-and-pencil arts of intelligence analysis rather than in the more physical arts of undercover work and arrest procedures. The decentralized structure of

the agency would have to be replaced with a more centralized one, perhaps an entirely centralized one, to minimize
the chance of regional needs obstructing national objectives.
Political superiors would have to be willing to tolerate low
performance levels, as measured by arrests and drug seizures, and to explain to a public worried about drug abuse
that there were good reasons not to invest in the production
of more arrests. Few of these changes have been proposed
by the agency; none would be easily achieved.

Because large conspiracy cases ordinarily will begin by
making a case against a particular drug dealer, any agency
seeking conspiracy cases must either have the ability to produce substantive (i.e., buy-and-bust) cases by itself or it
must have access to the defendants produced by other law
enforcement agencies so that they can be debriefed and
perhaps persuaded to become informants. The latter course
requires that police agencies be willing to share defendant-
informants, a policy that, with rare exceptions, never exists
and would be fiercely resisted. Informants are an investigator's chief resource; he is reluctant to share them with other
investigators in the same agency, to say nothing of sharing
them with other agencies. Thus, the DEA has adopted the
first course—namely, developing its own informants by
making street-level arrests. This policy has, in fact, permitted it to develop many important conspiracy cases, but at
the price of making many low-level buy-and-bust cases (thus
exposing it to criticism of the sort expressed by the Senate
subcommittee) and of developing an operational ethos that
rewards "door-kicking" agents who resist the kind of work
necessary to make conspiracy cases.[8]

DEA: Integrating Intelligence
and Enforcement

Because the informants and defendants necessary to initiate conspiracy investigations must be produced by the DEA if they are to be obtained at all, the distinctive competence or shared organizational mission of the agency has been defined by the work of the street-level narcotics agents—the instigators. The price one pays is the difficulty of exploiting cases beyond the initial arrest. The strategy by which the DEA has tried to cope with this problem is the division of labor between intelligence and investigative work—to create, that is, a group of employees with the special task of reviewing case records along with intelligence produced by other agencies (the FBI, the CIA) in order to provide information about the identity and operations of major trafficking organizations and to suggest linkages among otherwise unrelated cases that might lead to the development of multiple indictments or further, interregional investigations.

There is, of course, another kind of intelligence-gathering that can also be useful: recruiting informants from, or placing undercover agents in, major trafficking organizations and leaving them in place, under "deep cover," for extended periods in order to provide long-term tactical guidance rather than information for immediate arrests or seizures. This deployment is somewhat easier to carry out overseas, for abroad United States narcotics agents are not in theory supposed to make (and by and large do not make) arrests or seizures; instead, they are to advise host governments. There being little opportunity for instigative work, some overseas offices have turned to intelligence work of this sort. Furthermore, the value of such undercover work is greatest nearest the source of drug supplies—at the laboratory, for example—where there is the opportunity for the maximum disruption. Within the United States, deep-cover, long-term penetration of drug organizations has been less common.

The major organizational problem for the DEA, however, has been to create an effective information collation and analysis effort—"paper-and-pencil" intelligence—rather than to recruit productive deep-cover informants. The problem exists, essentially, because the dominant ethos of the agency, created and sustained by the central tasks of street-level investigators, does not provide a bureaucratic environment that nurtures, rewards, or pays heed to "paper-shufflers," including intelligence analysts.

The DEA has attempted to develop specialized intelligence units at both the regional and national levels. There are "regional intelligence units" in every regional office and there is at headquarters an office of intelligence that nominally has status equivalent to that of the office for enforcement. At neither level, however, is anyone satisfied with the results—agents regard most intelligence work, with a few important exceptions, as a waste of time, and intelligence analysts regard agents as narrow-minded and uncooperative. To the former, intelligence work supplies no useful product; to the latter, useful intelligence products are ignored.

The needs of case agents and of intelligence analysts, which one might suppose to be compatible if not identical, are in fact largely in conflict. At the local level, an agent wants immediate help, if he wants anything at all, on a pending case—looking up background information about a suspect or scanning files for lists of known confederates. To a regional intelligence analyst, this is "garbage work" involving mere clerical skills. The analyst would prefer to study files, many of them inactive, to try to discover, as one analyst put it, "a skeleton conspiracy case." The agents are skeptical that this longer view will produce anything of value and doubt whether by simply reading files any meaningful leads, of the sort that lead to recruiting good informants or making big buys, can be found.

The problem is made worse by the fact that a regional intelligence unit (RIU) is composed, in many instances, of civilians who have never been street agents or if agents, those who, in some cases, do not have good street records and have been put into an RIU because it is a "dumping ground." The RIU thus becomes a low-status unit the products of which are not taken seriously. In addition, street agents do not enjoy writing lengthy case reports and thus the information with which an RIU can work is often skimpy. If an RIU should offer a suggestion based on an incorrect inference from such reports, and the agents can immediately spot the weakness in the proposal based on their greater knowledge of suspects and informants, the credibility of the RIU sinks even lower.

At headquarters, the same problems are compounded by the fact that the office of enforcement has so little control over field investigations that it has little use for whatever intelligence might be produced. Moreover, the operating style and preferences of many professional intelligence officers is antithetical to that which agent supervisors prefer. Intelligence officers like to work with other intelligence officers and to be supervised by one of their own, just as agents prefer to work with and be supervised by fellow agents. This means that the former will resist the demands of the latter that intelligence and enforcement be merged under a single, enforcement-oriented administrator. Whether the merger would produce more useful products is not clear, but the desire for professional or occupational autonomy makes even achieving a merger quite difficult.

Many intelligence analysts acquire their experience in other agencies, such as the CIA, before coming to work for the DEA. In most intelligence organizations, the dominant principle of specialization is geographical. Analysts become *country* experts because, in agencies with political or military objectives, it is the behavior of another nation that is important. The need to master a foreign language reinforces the country orientation. The DEA, however, has little interest in the behavior of foreign governments or military powers, but has great interest in criminal organizations that operate across national boundaries. For the DEA, the relevant principle of specialization is by *commodity* (heroin, cocaine, amphetamines) or perhaps (if they can be identified) by type of trafficker. Within the DEA, a debate has raged over whether intelligence analysts should be organized around geographical regions (much preferred by many intelligence professionals) or around commodity systems (much preferred by agents).

In a few cases these obstacles are overcome. A "unified intelligence division" was created in one large regional office in which all narcotics information from the DEA and local police agencies was pooled. The El Paso Intelligence Center (EPIC) shares information from the DEA and the Customs Service regarding smuggling along the Southwest border. A headquarters unit on dangerous drugs, analyzing intelligence without regard to geographical assignment, was credited by several enforcement supervisors with providing invaluable aid to CENTACs working these cases.

But by and large, intelligence and investigation go their separate ways. The many factors that contribute to this divergence—the differences in tasks, in professional backgrounds, in time horizons, in principle of specialization—are institutionalized in the information-processing system of the organization. The traditional DEA reporting system grew directly out of the central task of street agents—making cases. The reports are stored, processed, and retrieved in ways that reflect that task. The files are, essentially, organized around the names of suspects, a procedure that makes eminently good sense to the extent the organization sees its mission to be supplying information for successful prosecutions. When a suspect is indicted, all the records about that suspect can be brought together and information in support of the indictment collated. Were intelligence the dominant mission of the agency, the files might well be organized around different principles—by kind of drug, by patterns of association, by means of transportation or communication, or by geographical area. Of course, there is no reason why a filing system cannot be cross-indexed in any number of ways. And of late, efforts have been made to do this. But the customary information system of the agency and its uses reveal the extent to which it is case, not systems, oriented, and that in turn reflects the agency's sense of its mission.

Administrative Issues in Perspective

Though administrators in both the FBI and the DEA are aware that there are important issues to be resolved if investigative agents are to be optimally managed, none of the initiatives described in this chapter altered in any important way the manner in which most agents selected and investigated their cases. The "Quality over Quantity" program in the FBI was welcomed by agents for the relief it offered from carrying trivial cases for statistical purposes, but since these cases had rarely been investigated seriously, no real changes in agent behavior occurred. The desire of headquarters to alter investigative priorities in a way that would favor greater attention being given to "white-collar" crimes made, at the field level, little difference except where an aggressive SAC was willing—at some risk—to reorganize the entire work force and to alter the way in which nonmaterial incentives (status) were distributed. The efforts by DEA administrators to produce more high-level conspiracy cases and to integrate the intelligence and investigative functions met with only modest success.

What each of these policies had in common—and they constitute, for the period covered by this research, the most important efforts at redirecting investigative work—was the inability of managers, especially at the headquarters level, to achieve a redefinition of the central tasks of the organizations' operators. Each of these efforts was based on an attempt to alter the *rules* under which the agents worked—reporting requirements, statistical measures, patterns of hierarchy, relations with other units—based on the assumption that the nature of the central task either could remain unchanged or would change spontaneously in conformity with the altered rules. The tasks of the operators did not, in fact, change, for the definition of these tasks derived from more fundamental considerations than those that managers could easily alter. These considerations included the fact that agents worked on the street alone or in pairs, had to develop routines for handling the interviewing and undercover features of their job in ways that were consistent with the realities of the situations in which they found themselves, and sought the approval and respect of fellow agents working in their office.

Administrative efforts to change operator behavior that fail to take into account the central tasks of these operators are likely to fail or to produce unintended results. FBI agents are essentially interviewers, DEA agents are instigators; trying to "fine tune" the performance of these tasks, especially from on high, is difficult at best.

Many of the recent changes in FBI rules and procedures—ending posting requirements, attempting to shift resource allocation decisions from a workload to a goal-oriented basis—had the desirable effect of lifting from the backs of investigators the burdens of useless paperwork and meaningless statistics that had once consumed considerable effort. These were, for the agents, popular changes. But to headquarters, it was not enough that agents had fewer burdens; what was sought was a redirection of their energies toward higher-quality or different kinds of cases. To accomplish this, however, required changes that headquarters alone could not make. They required the redefinition of tasks and of work groups at the local level, things that could be done (except *pro forma*) only by strong local leadership among SACs and first-line supervisors.

"Making a case" is the most common expression agents use to describe what they are doing. In time, one becomes so used to hearing it that one forgets how revealing it is. Once a case is "made"—which usually means, once it has been accepted for prosecution—the agent thinks of himself as having fulfilled his task. His *work* is by no means done—he must still fill out reports and appear in court—but "work" is simply energy expended and is not at all the same thing as "the job" (or, as used here, "the task"). Though agents often complain about uncooperative prosecutors, lenient judges, inadequate sentences, and the nature of the drug-trafficking problem, they do not evaluate themselves in terms of obtaining a certain sentence or having a particular impact on drug trafficking. They see themselves as "making cases" within the constraints—some useful, some bothersome, some stupid—created by the organization.

Thus, what appears as a paradox—that most members of the organization agree on the important tasks of the organization and agree on many of the ways in which the performance of those tasks falls short of expectations, yet act so as to ensure that the shortfall persists—is on closer inspection no paradox at all. It is, rather, the difference between individual opinion and collective action. FBI agents want to pursue important, rather than less important, cases, but higher-level efforts to define what is important strike the agents as mechanistic, unrealistic, or rigid. What they are saying is that, within broad limits, what is an important case is a matter of complex judgments that cannot easily be summarized into general propositions for purposes of supplying reports or understanding commands. DEA agents want to make Class I and II cases, but the very effort to define and measure these classes leads them to suppose that their behavior is being observed and measured and that therefore one must always seek to make *some* score, even if it is not the biggest one. Both FBI and DEA agents are affected by the opinions of their peers in ways that reinforce their tendency to do well those things that are part of the shared conception of the central task—namely, make cases.

Just as agents seek to assert and maintain their autonomy in the organization, managers also seek to maintain or expand the autonomy of the subunits for which they are responsible.[9] Though every level in an organization can, verbally, agree as to the mission of the organization and can identify many of the same problems that must be overcome to serve that mission, each level and each unit also must strive to obtain and keep those resources and that autonomy with which to make its contribution to the mission. But this means that when a higher-level manager, especially one who controls valuable resources, seeks to alter the behavior of a lower-level one or of operators generally, the lower-level units will be apprehensive. The RDs in the DEA and the SACs in the FBI both perceived the major management changes proposed by their superiors—the quality case program, the reduction in the emphasis on cocaine, the desire to incorporate intelligence units into field investigation, the demand for more attention to "white-collar" crime—in essentially maintenance terms, as possible threats to subunit autonomy and resources.

The closer the manager is to the operators, the more he tends to look at organizational rules as constraints within which he seeks to perform, or allow others to perform, essential tasks. The farther from the operators, the more the administrators regard these rules as ends in themselves. This is particularly the case when, as with the FBI and the DEA, there are few good measures of what operators are doing or how much of any given goal they are accomplishing. This is not simply another example of what

Robert Merton called "goal displacement"—the tendency of means to be viewed as ends.[10] It is, rather, a result of attempting to convert vaguely understood goals into task requirements at varying levels of generality. At the operators' level, these statements seem unrealistic or counterproductive; at the managers' level, they appear problematic and are frequently evaded; at the executives' level, they are statements of intention and aspiration.

CHAPTER

6

Executives

THE EXECUTIVE of an organization is that person or persons whose special responsibility is the maintenance of the organization.[1] By "maintenance" is not meant merely keeping the organization in being, but more generally assuring that the organization obtains the essential resources—money, personnel, clients, goodwill, political support—necessary for it to prosper as well as to survive. Threats to organizational maintenance can arise from external or internal sources. Externally, clients may go elsewhere, costs may rise, the media may become hostile, competitors may get the upper hand, or sources of financing may dry up. Internally, key employees may threaten to resign, workers may go on strike, morale may decline, or production may be interrupted.

All executives, public as well as private, are familiar with these problems. One might suppose that public, or governmental, executives have an easier time of it. After all, government agencies rarely go out of business or even face a serious threat to their existence. They are, if not immortal, then at least immune to the risks of bankruptcy that afflict ten thousand or so business firms each year.[2] In fact, however, a public bureaucracy exists in an especially difficult environment, one rife with threats to organizational well-being, and the public executive must cope with these stresses having, ordinarily, weaker and fewer powers than those of his private counterpart.

The public executive cannot freely alter his organization's goals, reallocate its factors of production, or acquire at his discretion additional resources. The goals (at least in general terms), the resources, and the utilization of facilities (and, to a substantial degree, even of personnel) are defined or authorized by political institutions—legislatures, courts, presidents, governors—whose support is contingent and conditional.[3] It is contingent in that it may be withdrawn, altered, or reduced at any time, often without recourse or appeal (a bureau chief cannot sue a budget examiner or an appropriations committee chairman for breach of contract). It is conditional in that obtaining it at all requires the executive to accept a long and growing list of constraints on his authority—civil service rules governing the hiring, assigning, and firing of personnel, accounting rules governing the uses to which money may be put, freedom of information laws designed to minimize his opportunities for acting in secret or maintaining confidential records, and so on.

While government bureaus tend to survive even when they manage their maintenance problems poorly, bureau executives do not. They are judged daily, and harshly, on the basis of reputation as much or more than achievements and with little regard for the limitations of their powers. For the typical public executive, organizational life is a series of crises—real, anticipated, or imagined threats to the well-being of the organization or the executive himself arising from the unstable environment in which the organization is located.

The consequence of this is that such an executive will devote a large part of his time to coping with the political environment rather than the internal management of the organization. His daily calendar will be dominated by the need to respond to press criticisms, to testify before congressional committees, to serve on interagency committees composed (in part) of real or potential rivals, and to meet with a variety of persons who can affect the budget, reputation, and powers of his agency.[4] The only way this crisis-orientation can be minimized is by devising some way of assuring the autonomy of the agency. An agency is autonomous to the degree it can act independently of some or all of the groups that have the authority to constrain it. Autonomy is acquired by eliminating rival organizations that might wish to perform some or all of the same tasks as one's own bureau and by acquiring sufficient goodwill and prestige as to make attacks on oneself or one's agency costly for one's critics.

In my view, it is the desire for autonomy, and not for large budgets, new powers, or additional employees, that is the dominant motive of public executives. In the conventional view, a government bureaucracy is "imperialistic"—it steadily strives for more resources and additional authority because to do so will enhance the income and prestige of the bureaucrats.[5] There is little doubt that, other things being equal, bureau chiefs would like more money and no doubt at all that they feel their authority is not adequate to their responsibilities. But as Marc Tipermas has shown in his study of federal executive branch reorganizations, when confronted with a choice, many if not most bureaus prefer greater autonomy to greater resources.[6] Morton Halperin comes to the same conclusion in explaining the otherwise paradoxical fact that the heads of the military services disliked Secretary of Defense Robert S. McNamara, even though during his tenure their budgets rose rapidly, while they approved of Secretary of Defense Melvin Laird, even though he cut their budgets.[7] McNamara lessened service autonomy, Laird increased it.

The essential difference between the FBI and the DEA, viewed from the perspective of their executives, is that the former agency was able to establish a high degree of au-

tonomy and the latter was not. The autonomy of the FBI was
substantially reduced in the mid-1970s as a result of revelations regarding illegal entries and electronic surveillances at
a time when public opinion had come to be generally dis-
trustful of public institutions and less responsive to concerns
for domestic security, but until then—which is to say, for
over forty-five years—the FBI enjoyed an almost unparal-
leled degree of autonomy. This is not to say the Bureau
acted without regard for the wishes of its constitutional superiors; quite the contrary. Part of the reason it achieved such
substantial freedom from criticism or threats to its resources
or powers is that it anticipated the needs and cultivated the
support of key elected officials, chiefly congressmen. Those
who were later to suggest that somehow the Bureau had
achieved its power by duping, ignoring, or intimidating
Congress have simply not read, or have misread, the histori-
cal record. At one time, narcotics law enforcement, in the
form of the old Federal Bureau of Narcotics, enjoyed substantial autonomy, but never to the extent of the FBI and in
recent years—for about the last two decades—scarcely at all.
The implications for the internal management of the FBI
and the DEA of this difference in autonomy have been
profound.

Maintaining the FBI

The great achievement of J. Edgar Hoover was to convert a
weak, corrupt, partisan investigative agency into one that
never experienced a serious scandal and enjoyed widespread, bipartisan public confidence. The story of his acces-
sion to the office of director at the age of twenty-nine has
been frequently told;[8] admirers and critics alike agree that

he utterly transformed a disgraceful bureau into a modern investigative agency in which personnel were selected on merit alone, held to the most exacting standards of behavior, ruthlessly punished at the first sign of improper or partisan behavior, and supported with a remarkable system of files, fingerprint records, and scientific laboratories.

In 1924, as in 1974, a major issue involved the manner in which the Justice Department was investigating domestic security cases. The old Bureau of Investigation, in which Hoover was a young official, had been deeply involved in rounding up, under the direction of Attorney General A. Mitchell Palmer, thousands of real and alleged radicals. Many were recent immigrants, most were arrested without warrants, and most were eventually released without punishment. The "Red scare" of 1919–20, though popular in some quarters, brought the Bureau of Investigation into disrepute, especially after a Senate investigating committee confirmed the illegality of many of the raids.

In 1924, as again fifty years later, there were also charges of illegal surreptitious entries, wiretaps, and surveillances conducted in part for political purposes. William J. Burns, founder of the detective agency bearing his name, was the Bureau's director in the Harding administration at a time when agents harassed political opponents of Attorney General Harry Dougherty, used force to obtain confessions, kept files on the partisan affiliations of individual agents, and appointed agents (some with criminal records) on the basis of their political connections among congressmen. And the Bureau was instrumental in breaking a strike among railroad workers.

Hoover moved swiftly to eliminate corruption and incompetence and to improve the public image as well as the professional performance of the renamed Federal Bureau of Investigation. His charter was a six-point Memorandum of Understanding issued by Attorney General Harlan Fiske Stone, who appointed Hoover, that limited the FBI to fact-gathering regarding violations of federal law; it was "not concerned with political or other opinions of individuals" but "only with their conduct, and then only with such conduct as is forbidden by the laws of the United States."[9] He fired the hacks, required college degrees with legal or accounting training for new agents, established the famous inspection system, kept agents out of the civil service system so they could be fired summarily for misconduct, directed that all files and records were to be held in strict confidence, and politely told congressmen attempting to interfere in the appointment or assignment of agents that he was "unable to accede to your interest."[10]

These moves, coupled with the FBI's role in solving various celebrated crimes such as the Lindbergh kidnapping, in capturing or killing gangsters such as John Dillinger, "Baby Face" Nelson, "Pretty Boy" Floyd, "Ma" Barker, and Alvin Karpis, and in penetrating Nazi espionage efforts during World War II, made the Bureau perhaps the most popular agency in the entire federal government. Resisting the particularistic demands of individual congressmen and politicians, though seemingly a risky policy by the political standards of the 1920s, proved in time to be a most successful posture as the Bureau earned the prestige that made every congressman both respectful of its stature and eager to enhance it further. A later generation would question whether flamboyant Midwestern gangsters such as Dillinger or Barker deserved to be called "Public Enemy Number 1" in view of the more insidious and better-organized threat posed by the emergent criminal syndicates and would suggest that the Bureau's role in solving the Lindbergh kidnapping case and in apprehending the eight Nazi saboteurs who landed on the Long Island coast was, in fact, rather marginal, but at the time few doubted that the "G-Men" deserved all the credit they were getting and more.[11]

If the theory of "bureaucratic imperialism" were true, one

would expect an agency as successful and as popular as the FBI to grow rapidly, not only in resources, but in jurisdiction and power. Hoover, to be sure, was never reluctant to ask for the funds he believed he needed, but there is little evidence that he sought to enlarge his jurisdiction or monopolize federal law enforcement. He refused for decades to become deeply involved in investigating organized crime, and he resisted until the mid-1960s any extensive investigation of civil rights violations except for those perpetrated by the Ku Klux Klan, which he detested. When President Franklin D. Roosevelt suggested that the FBI take responsibility for press censorship during World War II, Hoover demurred.[12] When the United States Army made plans at the outbreak of World War II to evacuate Japanese-Americans from California cities and confine them in isolated "relocation camps," Hoover, far from leaping at the chance to investigate alleged Nisei subversives, opposed the plan and asserted that there was no evidence of such subversion.[13] He opposed allowing the FBI to take over the investigation of narcotics trafficking even when prominent congressmen and influential White House aides favored the merger. He steadfastly opposed the notion of a "national police force" and, under this banner, would scotch various plans in Congress to extend the Bureau's jurisdiction in unwanted directions.[14] During the Nixon administration he opposed the so-called "Huston Plan" for a coordinated, illegal governmental attack on domestic radicals.[15]

A cynical interpretation could be offered for all these positions: Hoover stayed out of civil rights cases because he did not like blacks or because he wanted to keep good relations with Southern congressmen; he avoided narcotics and organized crime because he feared the corruption of his agents; he shunned the Nisei relocation and the Huston Plan because other agencies, rather than the Bureau, would play the leading role. There is some truth in these explanations, though they fail to account for certain dramatic changes—for example, the zeal with which the Bureau went after organized crime figures and violators of civil rights once Hoover decided to move in these areas. The most important fact, however, is to be found in what all these actions have in common. Throughout his rule, Hoover acted so as to protect the autonomy of the FBI by resisting any effort to change or add to the central tasks his agents were performing and by opposing collaborative ventures with other agencies that were or might become rivals.

Hoover knew instinctively what every natural executive knows: having a monopoly position on even a small piece of turf is better than having a competitive position on a large one. Just as Hoover resisted the Nisei evacuation and the Huston plan because they required collaboration, so also he opposed allowing FBI agents to serve as members of Justice Department "strike forces" sent to cities to root out political corruption and attack organized crime. Hoover was more than willing to investigate such matters, at least after the mid-1960s, but never willing to allow his agents to become subordinate to other leaders, even to other leaders in the Justice Department itself. So, too, did he firmly resist sharing FBI informants with any other agency; he was happy to supply *leads* from these informants to other agencies, as the Bureau has done for years in narcotics cases, but not the informants themselves.

Hoover changed his enforcement policies only when it was clear there would be a net benefit to the Bureau. Looking into organized crime *did* expose agents to risks of corruption, and assigning high priority to civil rights matters *did* cause friction with some Southern law enforcement agencies (but not, so far as we know, with Southern congressmen). But when Robert F. Kennedy, the brother of President John F. Kennedy, was attorney general and when popular concern over civil rights and organized crime was obviously high, the costs to the Bureau of resisting the new policies had clearly become greater than the risks of compliance.[16]

Hoover refused, however, to change Bureau policy when the central tasks of the agents would have to be altered. Narcotics investigation meant turning agents into instigators, working undercover in situations that required one to emulate, if not adopt, the language, style, and values of the criminal world. Not only would this expose agents to temptations involving money and valuable narcotics, it would also require them to engage in enforcement policies that, though legal, struck many citizens as unsavory. And perhaps most important, the key asset of the agent—public acceptance and confidence—might be weakened as the agent's image changed from that of a bank clerk or insurance salesman to that of a habitué of "street life." The white-shirt, black-shoe, blue-suit appearance of the typical agent has been the source of much humor, yet Hoover realized from the outset that strict conformity to prevailing standards of propriety was essential for an organization that depended on public confidence more than anything else. As John P. Mohr, for long a key administrator in the FBI, put it, "You knew what a special agent looked like. You were proud of him. You could trust him."[17] After Hoover, the dress code of the Bureau was modified slightly, but always in keeping with prevailing Middle American standards.

Hoover was, as Joseph Kraft once called him with grudging admiration, "the complete bureaucrat," or as Sanford Ungar put it in a generally critical book, an organizational "genius."[18] He created and led the most centrally directed, rigidly hierarchical civilian bureaucracy in the federal government, one that was privately the envy of other bureau chiefs struggling with civil service regulations, employee unions, and skeptical congressmen. Much of the study of American public administration consists of scholarly accounts of why and how large bureaucracies defeat the hopes of their leaders by distorting communications, forming external alliances, leaking information to the media, and identifying with local clients at the expense of organizational loyalty. The story of the FBI stands in sharp contrast to these accounts. Though FBI agents sometimes did things that bore no apparent relationship to any reasonable organizational goal, they did not act contrary to the wishes of their boss except when they were confident they could do so undetected, and then only with considerable anxiety.[19]

The managerial devices by which autonomy and central authority were protected have been described in chapters 4 and 5. The only statistics kept by the Bureau were "statistical accomplishments," and these were defined so as to guarantee that each year would show more "accomplishments" than the preceding one. In March 1972, Hoover made his last appearance before the House Subcommittee on Appropriations (it was, ironically, also the last FBI budget hearing to be presided over by Congressman John J. Rooney of New York, for years the scourge of the State Department and friend of the Bureau). Two months later, Hoover was dead, but his performance in March was a vintage example of the art of impressing legislators. In reporting on the field investigative operations of the Bureau during the 1971 fiscal year, Hoover was able, as usual, to report "record" accomplishments—"a record 221,940 matters" were pending investigation; "convictions . . . reached a new peak of 13,357"; "a record 33,863 fugitives were located"; "another record was set with the recovery of 32,076 automobiles"; "a new peak was reached as fines, savings and recoveries totaled "$475,074,108"; "a new high of 631 convictions of hoodlum, gambling and vice figures" were obtained.[20]

Criticisms of such statistics had begun to be heard, and at the outset of the hearings Congressman Rooney took cognizance of that fact:

MR. ROONEY.   One Carolyn Lewis, of CBS radio, said you [Hoover] bring some phony statistics up here and we are swayed to appropriate everything you ask for as a result of your putting it over on us.
    Well, you and I know we have kidded about those statistics for

many years. Some of them we depend upon as a real indication of
what you do, particularly the one with regard to the number of un-
compensated hours of overtime which the Bureau employees put in.
That is a very competent statistic.

We know when a car is recovered that at least six agencies participate in the credit for it, and when it comes to fines and recoveries
we know that there are at least five agencies which participate in the
credit for that. There is nothing wrong with that. We were never
hoodwinked by anything done here, I assure you, because I think all
the Members of this Committee are a bit hardboiled. We look with a
jaundiced eye at everything that is presented to us from the time we
start the hearing.[21]

And, indeed, the subcommittee was not being hoodwinked. What led it, year in and year out, to recommend
that the Bureau receive at least as much money as it wanted
was not any simple bedazzlement with "record accomplishments," but its confidence in the Bureau's integrity, its belief in its mission, its sympathy for the director's ideology,
and (last but not least) the absence of any bureaucratic rival
to the FBI that might dispute its claims or challenge its authority. It liked to hear of the Bureau's accomplishments
because it both confirmed its own judgment and provided it
(and the Bureau) with a strong public record to justify its
confidence. More revealing of the sources of at least some
subcommittee members' support for the FBI was this re-
mark by Chairman Rooney at the beginning of the 1972
hearings:

We are honored to have with us this morning the distinguished Director of the Federal Bureau of Investigation, the Honorable J. Edgar
Hoover. I would like to say to him that he seems to thrive, as far as his
appearance is concerned here today, on the barbs of these left-wing
foul balls who have been trying to lay a glove on him. I don't think anybody has succeeded up to now.

MR. HOOVER.   Mr. Chairman, I have a philosophy. You are honored by your friends and you are distinguished by your enemies. I have
been very distinguished.[22]

When Clarence Kelley launched what was later called the
"quality case program" in 1975, it was generally feared

within the Bureau that this would lead to a drop in caseloads that would in turn cause congressional criticism and perhaps even a budget cut. Many SACs who opposed the new program used this possibility as their major argument against it. In fact, no such adverse effects occurred. The House Appropriations Subcommittee gave no indication it was at all disturbed by Kelley's statement, in the 1976 hearings, that the FBI had received 10 percent fewer investigative matters in fiscal 1975 than in the preceding year as a result, in part, of the Bureau's desire to "allocate increased resources to the more significant matters."[23] Perhaps to be on the safe side, Kelley went on to point out that "FBI accomplishments reached record levels in many instances."[24] Most of the questions of the subcommittee members, in 1976 as in previous years, had to do with interesting cases in which the Bureau was involved and general philosophies of law enforcement. When the 1978 appropriations hearings were held, Kelley felt sufficiently confident of congressional reaction to omit the usual litany about "record accomplishments" and instead to speak candidly about decreases in "some of the traditional workload and accomplishment indicators" in accordance with the quality case program and the recommendations of the General Accounting Office.[25] He noted the increased emphasis on "white-collar" and organized crime investigations but admitted that as yet there was "no way to precisely measure the benefits of this change in investigative emphasis."[26]

The emphasis on statistical accomplishments never took the form of comparing FBI results with crime rates. What *proportion* of FBI-investigated matters was solved or produced arrests and convictions was rarely, if ever, a subject of discussion with Congress. Though the statistics used had little meaning by themselves, and though a decline in these statistics in the post-Hoover period produced no adverse political reaction, the drive to produce these numbers remained intense until 1975–76. This pressure was part of a managerial strategy designed to prevent criticism, cultivate public support, and ensure strict standards of integrity.

The strategy included rigid personnel controls, a centralized promotional system, and investigative rules designed primarily to ensure that the work would be up-to-date and immune to charges of sloppiness or incompleteness. Among the personnel controls were, of course, the famous dress code and the personal grooming standards, one of which became part of a lawsuit brought by a discharged male clerk (not an agent) in the fingerprint section who had been fired for wearing long hair. (The clerk claimed he was the victim of sex discrimination, since female but not male clerks were allowed to wear their hair long. He lost.) In addition the *FBI Handbook* prohibits agents from making speeches on "controversial topics" without Bureau approval, buying or selling securities "for speculation," engaging in political activity (except voting), and uttering public expressions of opinion on the "efficiency or standing" of present or former FBI employees. At one time no agent was allowed to drink coffee in a public place because, so the story goes, a citizen had complained to his congressman in the early years of the Bureau about seeing federal agents "loafing" at a time when the FBI's prestige was still precarious. Hoover swiftly decided that no citizen would ever again have those grounds for complaint, and public coffee-drinking while on duty ended.

The centralized disciplinary and promotional system ensured not that all cases would be handled in the same way or that each field office would have the same investigative priorities but rather that everyone seeking to rise in the Bureau would have a Bureau—which is to say, a headquarters—point of view. Administrative advancement required frequent changes in duty assignment, extended tours at headquarters, close evaluation, and abandoning direct investigative work in favor of paperwork. A key step in this promotion process was the time spent as an Inspector's Aide—part of the "goon squad"—that audited in painstaking detail each field office. The experience guaranteed that every future SAC knew the organization's rules and the consequences of their violation.

As explained in chapter 4, this centralized personnel and inspectional system led some observers to conclude, erroneously, that the Bureau had centralized case management. In fact, the system ensured only the central management of case*loads*—every agent had roughly the same number of cases (at least on paper). But the agents were very much on their own when it came to conducting investigations. And far from producing a set of investigative priorities, the emphasis on caseloads, statistical accomplishments, and posting rules meant that there would be *no* priorities except when a "big" (i.e., nationally significant) case broke or except as Hoover decided to emphasize some kinds of intelligence or proactive investigations (such as domestic security cases) that could be made subject to central control.

The massive investigative caseloads of the domestic security squads, before they were drastically reduced under Kelley, are an apt illustration of the consequences for agents of a managerial system based in large part on ensuring the maintenance and enhancement of the Bureau and its director. It is important not to be misunderstood here. I do not claim that the FBI became involved in domestic security matters simply to enhance its organizational position. Nor do I doubt that its involvement stemmed in part from what some critics have described as Hoover's "frenzied concern" for radicals.[27] And I recognize that the generally conservative political views of most FBI personnel would contribute to their willingness to keep close tabs on "extremists." There are some real, not imaginary, domestic threats to security, civil rights, and democratic processes: the Ku Klux Klan, the Symbionese Liberation Army, the Black Panthers (or at least one faction at one time), the Weather Underground, and various other groups that shoot, bomb, lynch, or disrupt. One expects (and perhaps wants) the head of a law enforcement agency to have a broader definition of what constitutes a potential threat to security than would a judge or a civil liberties lawyer. What needs explaining is not that the FBI was involved with domestic security cases or that Hoover and his associates were political conservatives, but why the Bureau investigated so widely and often so indiscriminately.

As the General Accounting Office concluded in its report on the matter, the FBI, "rather than concentrating on the most violence-prone groups," has "diffused its domestic intelligence investigative coverage to the point where many investigations do not lead to positive results."[28] What is all the more remarkable, given Hoover's typically scrupulous regard for ensuring that he had solid legal authority for any action he proposed to take, was the fact that for several decades the FBI could rely only on a Bureau interpretation of a 1936 memorandum by Hoover summarizing a conversation he had with President Roosevelt and on subsequent presidential orders by Roosevelt, Harry S. Truman, and Dwight D. Eisenhower. These directives, while they may well authorize investigation of communist and fascist groups, hardly seemed to cover surveillance of women's liberation, antiwar, and civil rights organizations. The normally cautious Hoover, always alert to cover his flanks, seemed to violate his own best instincts in this matter.

I suggest three explanations. First, though Congress never passed legislation explicitly giving the Bureau comprehensive statutory authority for domestic security cases, virtually every key congressman knew and approved of what the FBI was doing. By the standards of the 1930s, 1940s, 1950s, and even the 1960s, it would have struck most congressmen as ludicrous for anyone to suggest that the Bureau had only tenuous legal grounds for keeping tabs on radicals, loosely defined. Second, for the Bureau not to compile the fullest possible files on individuals with suspect affiliations would have seriously undercut its preeminent organizational position in official Washington. The FBI receives requests from the White House, Congress, the military, and other federal agencies for "name checks" on individuals being considered for appointments and for accounts of the intentions and activities of various extremist organizations. It would be unthinkable for the Bureau to say, in response to these inquiries, that it did not know the answer, or did not care to find out, or that its priorities were such that finding out anything about the named individuals would have to wait. To even imply such a response would be to invite the creation of rival programs by other agencies to supply the answers. Finally, the managerial style of Hoover was such that few agents ever wished to find themselves in the position of answering a question from the director by saying, "I don't know."

The result of these organizational and political factors, taken in combination with normal bureaucratic routines that make file-keeping a way of life and the widespread view among most Americans and virtually all agents that domestic security was a proper object for Bureau activity, was that domestic security cases were opened with few, if any, guidelines that would help distinguish between the more and less important. Headquarters did not directly supervise most routine domestic security investigations any more than it supervised most criminal investigations, but it had ample means to make certain that *work* was being done. Thus, when the New York field office suggested in April 1975 that it cease overseeing the Eldridge Cleaver faction of the Black Panther Party because it had virtually ceased to exist, headquarters disagreed and insisted the case be kept open. When other field offices proposed removing certain individuals from a list of persons constituting an actual or potential threat to domestic security (the administrative index, or ADEX), headquarters disagreed.[29] It is hard to say whether the field or headquarters made the correct judgment. The important point, however, is that it was the normal disposition of headquarters to resolve all doubts in favor of long lists, full investigations, and new cases, and it was the task of the inspectors to ensure that local files were "complete" and up-to-date. It should come as no surprise, therefore, that the field believed that the only acceptable statement of priorities was "do everything."

In all this, it is essential to bear in mind that maintaining a governmental organization does not occur in a vacuum. What constitutes a successful maintenance strategy depends crucially on the prevailing sentiments of key political actors, and for the FBI, with its policy of building grass-roots support directly through publicity and a visible record of accomplishment, "key political actors" included public opinion generally. Throughout virtually all of Hoover's administration, the mission of the FBI was fully consistent with public expectations, beliefs, and values.

When those expectations and beliefs changed, as they did in the mid-1970s, the maintenance problem of the Bureau became more complicated and its autonomy, for the first time, was seriously threatened. An acting director of the FBI, L. Patrick Gray III, had been charged with being complicit in, or at least casual about, the Watergate coverup.[30] The use by the FBI of illegal, surreptitious entries directed against radical organizations had been revealed. The role of the FBI in conducting political inquiries for the White House under both Democratic and Republican administrations was disclosed. Under the Freedom of Information Act, private citizens were for the first time obtaining access to FBI files about them and their organizations. The National Crime Information Center (NCIC), a computerized record of stolen property, wanted persons, and criminal histories to which local police departments have access, became controversial among persons concerned about individual rights to privacy. The existence of the COINTELPRO effort to disrupt, harass, and discredit dissident organizations was divulged, and numerous lawsuits were brought against the FBI. In some suits, individual FBI agents were named as

codefendants, making them personally liable should the suit
be decided in favor of the plaintiff. The electronic surveillance directed against Dr. Martin Luther King, Jr., the
civil rights leader, and his organization, the Southern Chris-
tian Leadership Conference, was revealed (as well as the fact
that Attorney General Robert F. Kennedy approved the
taps), and additional charges were made that the FBI sought
privately to discredit Dr. King.[31]

The magnitude of the task facing a political executive
when his or his organization's position is threatened was
made abundantly clear to Kelley. Between February 1974
and August 1976, Kelley and his principal associates testified
at least forty-six times before various congressional committees. An appearance might well consume an entire day;
more important, preparation for each appearance, and answering subsequent questions from the press stimulated by
the hearings, as well as retrieving files for and replying to
written inquiries from the committees, could take several
days. And because more than one committee was involved,
most issues had to be gone over several times: for the House
Appropriations Subcommittee; the Senate Judiciary Subcommittee on Constitutional Rights; the Senate Select Committee on Intelligence; the House Judiciary Subcommittee
on Courts, Civil Liberties, and the Administration of Justice;
the House Committee on Internal Security; the House Government Operations Subcommittee on Foreign Operations;
the Senate Appropriations Committee; the Senate Foreign
Relations Committee; the Senate Government Operations
Permanent Subcommittee on Investigations; the House Post
Office and Civil Service Committee's Subcommittee on
Postal Facilities, Mail, and Labor Management; the Senate
Judiciary Subcommittee on Internal Security; the House
Subcommittee on Housing and Consumer Interests; the
House Committee on Small Business; . . . and others.[32]

The unchallenged prestige of the FBI, the basis for its ex-
traordinary autonomy, collapsed utterly, and congressmen

who had once attended hearings at which Hoover testified in order to congratulate him and bask in his reflected glory now eagerly sought forums in which they could join in attacking his record and the behavior of his successors. In the decentralized structure of the United States Congress, the only limit on the number of power centers with which a controversial bureau must do business is the parliamentary imagination of 535 individual legislators. A political executive may complain of the impossibility of simultaneously satisfying so many masters, but to no avail; the system works this way, not merely because legislators like it, but because that is how the framers of the Constitution designed it.

A bureau in trouble becomes fair game for rivals wishing to assert their authority. Review of the FBI budget by the Department of Justice became exceptionally close. The Office of Management and Budget was able to compel the Bureau to accept a reduction in agent personnel. Guidelines for the use of informants, the opening of domestic security cases, and the conduct of foreign counterintelligence cases were drafted by the attorney general (with participation, but at a disadvantage, by FBI officials) and imposed on the Bureau. There was even a suggestion, unthinkable in Hoover's time, that the Department of Justice might demand use of some of the parking spaces beneath the new FBI headquarters building.

The impact of this change in organizational autonomy on the behavior of agents is difficult to assess. Agents from various parts of the country with whom I spoke indicated that in the "heartland," outside such areas as New York City or San Francisco, public support for the Bureau remained high and thus the ability of agents to conduct interviews, its essential resource, was not adversely affected. But where agents were expected to do something more complex than talking to people, there was a tendency by agents to demand written instructions from the highest level in order to protect themselves from the possibility of subsequent criticism.

The weakened political position of the Bureau did not cause the changes in organizational rules, statistics, and priorities—these arose out of Kelley's own convictions reinforced by the views of his immediate staff—but the Bureau's reduced autonomy did make it possible for those changes to be taken seriously. Kelley's proposals could not, in the circumstances of the mid-1970s, be resisted successfully by opponents within the Bureau on the grounds that the old ways had always worked; or that congressional support should not be jeopardized by untested innovations; or that any change would imply criticism of the past. In short, a crisis in autonomy was a necessary though not a sufficient condition for organizational change. Ironically, however, this same crisis impeded the implementation of the change because it diverted the energies of top Bureau executives toward external maintenance problems; it drained the resources available for carrying through on new ideas; and it made some lower-ranking managers and even street agents apprehensive about accepting the greater responsibility that Kelley sought to give them.

There can be little doubt, however, that the challenges to the Bureau's autonomy also weakened the powers of the headquarters Old Guard. The dominance of the old Administrative Division was slowly eroded and the rules-oriented Inspection Division was combined with the change-oriented Office of Planning and Evaluation. The associate director and the two key assistants to the director were removed. Indeed, if anything, Kelley moved too slowly in making these top personnel changes and thus may have delayed longer than was necessary the steps that he wanted to take to restore public confidence and press forward his managerial changes.

Maintaining the DEA

The Drug Enforcement Administration has not in recent years been able to achieve or maintain the degree of autonomy enjoyed by the FBI. Though the old Federal Bureau of Narcotics, especially under the leadership of the redoubtable Harry Anslinger, enjoyed considerable prestige, by the mid-1960s it was merged with another agency and transferred out of the Treasury Department and into the Justice Department after it had become tainted with scandal. Its successor bodies—the Bureau of Narcotics and Dangerous Drugs and the DEA—have been plagued with bureaucratic rivals, especially the Customs Service and local police departments, and have had to endure unremitting criticism from within the Justice Department, from congressmen, and from certain broad sectors of public opinion. The lot of their various executives has not been a happy one.

Despite this, the DEA (and before it, the BNDD) has enjoyed success in obtaining appropriations. Richard Fenno, in his study of the appropriations process in Congress, found that the Narcotics Bureau, over a sixteen-year period, was one of those agencies, like the FBI, the Extension Service, and the Forest Service, that got from the House Appropriations Committee almost all it asked for in the way of funds.[33] Few congressmen have been willing to vote against money for arresting drug traffickers, whatever their other concerns about the success or the tactics of the bureau. A staff member of the House Subcommittee that handles both FBI and DEA appropriations remarked to an interviewer that it was rare for the DEA to be criticized or its budget seriously challenged (and, of course, unheard of for the FBI to experience such treatment). During the hearing in March 1975 on the fiscal 1976 budget, some sharp, critical questions were asked of then-Administrator John R. Bartels, Jr., but the committee staff later remarked that this was unusual.[34]

The DEA experience supports the view that the problem of autonomy is different from, and sometimes unrelated to, the problem of resources. And the experience of the administrators of the DEA suggests that for these executives, autonomy has been the chief difficulty.

The inability of the DEA to establish its own domain or autonomy is in part the result of the nature of its task. It does not detect crime, it instigates it in order to apprehend offenders who unwittingly break laws in full view of law enforcement agents. To the average citizen, even those who heartily endorse a vigorous program of drug law enforcement, the task seems rather unsavory and certainly not as wholesome as tracking down an unknown violent criminal by feats of "scientific detection." And to skeptics of drug enforcement, the task verges on entrapment and perhaps even contributes to the evil it seeks to prevent. And even supporters of the program concede that the task exposes agents to great risks of corruption.

At one time, criticism of the drug enforcement task was scarcely heard because the nature of that task was not fully understood (most people probably thought narcotics agents and FBI agents did essentially the same things) and because drug traffickers were thought to be (and perhaps largely were) confined to small numbers of outcast or low-status parts of society—Mexican immigrants who smuggled in marijuana, Chinese immigrants who used opium, black jazz musicians who sniffed cocaine or injected heroin.[35] "Reefer madness," "opium dens," and Negro addicts of the sort portrayed in George Gershwin's *Porgy 'n Bess* were remote threats and merely another manifestation, or so people thought, of the generally sordid conditions of outcast life. In the 1960s, the public became aware that drug abuse reached all walks of life, that it involved white schoolchildren as well as black ones, and that drug experimentation and drug abuse were rising rapidly. This had, I conjecture, contradictory effects: it produced a greater sense of public urgency about the problem, but it also sensitized public opinion to the possibility that "decent," i.e., middle-class, citizens would be entrapped, "busted," "stigmatized." The handwriting was on the wall for narcotics agents when large numbers of persons stopped using the phrase "dope fiend" and started talking about "victimless crimes."

In addition, the DEA and its predecessor agencies were never able to gain monopoly control over narcotics law enforcement or over the information systems used to measure the extent of the problem and, by implication, the success of the agency. The Customs Service had always been in charge of detecting the movement of contraband, including drugs, across United States borders. In pursuit of this task, it hired not only baggage and cargo inspectors but agents who worked abroad (developing intelligence, cooperating with foreign customs agents) and domestically (tracking down suspected smugglers). The Federal Bureau of Narcotics could not take over this task—it is almost impossible, technologically or organizationally, to divide the detection of smuggling across borders between drug and non-drug contraband. So long as the FBN was located in the same cabinet department (Treasury) as Customs, such conflicts as arose were manageable. But when the FBN moved to Justice, only cabinet-level discussions presided over by the president of the United States could resolve the policy disputes that erupted, and naturally a president can only give, at best, a small fraction of his time and political power to the resolution of such messy arguments.

In addition, there was a large—and in the 1960s, a rapidly growing—bureaucracy that saw the narcotics issues as a problem of public health rather than law enforcement. Indicators of drug abuse were developed by doctors, based at first on death rates among known addicts and later on measuring rates of serum hepatitis (to which young heroin users are especially prone) among hospital admittees and on detecting opiate derivatives in the urine of arrested persons. Whereas the FBI could show that a rising crime rate (calculated from figures it compiled) was matched by a rising level of investigations, convictions, fines, savings, and recoveries, the DEA and before it the BNDD could at best show some increase in arrests and drug seizures in the face of an independently measured rate of drug abuse that was increasing at an epidemic rate. Furthermore, while no one would argue that arresting a bank robber led to the commission of more bank robberies, many persons could and did argue that arresting drug users and dealers, by driving up the price of a drug for which the demand was supposedly inelastic, led addicts to steal and rob to pay for their habits.[36] The DEA was caught either way. It could not arrest dealers or seize supplies fast enough to satisfy those who thought that getting tough was the best solution to drug abuse, and it arrested too many dealers and users to please those who thought that keeping drug use illegal only made matters worse.

During the 1960s, crime and drug abuse became highly political issues. But whereas the argument over "crime in the streets" left the FBI, if anything, stronger, more aggressive, and better endowed with resources, it left the BNDD shaky and beleaguered. The FBI was announcing "record" and "peak" accomplishments when crime was rising; it was rewarded with more manpower and funds. The BNDD was investigating some complex international drug-trafficking systems in ways that led to comparatively few arrests. The BNDD defended its policy by explaining that its job was not to arrest street dealers but instead to build cases against the leaders of drug syndicates. The Nixon administration was not satisfied and created a rival agency, the Office of Drug Abuse Law Enforcement (ODALE) headed by Myles Ambrose, a vigorous and colorful former Customs chief. It quickly began arresting street dealers and hauling them before federal grand juries where, given immunity against prosecution, it was hoped they would implicate more dealers.

And as if this were not enough, Reorganization Plan Number 2 of 1973 was sent to Congress. The BNDD would be combined with part of the Customs Service and given a new name (DEA) and, as it turned out, a new executive. The object was to eliminate the bureaucratic rivalry between Customs and the BNDD.

Some observers find conspiracies where I find only ambition and rivalry. Edward Jay Epstein claims that the various reorganizations and bureaucratic power plays involving narcotics law enforcement during the Nixon administration were nothing less than an attempted *coup d'état:* "Under the aegis of a 'war on heroin,' " he writes, a series of new offices, such as ODALE, were set up to perform "the functions of 'the Plumbers' on a far grander scale."[37] A plan by G. Gordon Liddy to set up a special narcotics unit reporting directly to the White House was actually, Epstein suggests, a proposal to gather political intelligence "under the cloak of combatting the drug menace."[38] This plan later became ODALE, ostensibly a narcotics law enforcement agency but in reality a "White House-controlled investigative unit" that was to function as a "private police force" designed to help "seize power within the federal government."[39] The DEA was, according to Epstein, supposed to be the "strong investigative arm for domestic surveillance that President Nixon had long quested after."[40]

Epstein offers ample evidence of political grandstanding about the heroin problem, of pervasive bureaucratic infighting among BNDD, ODALE, and Customs, and of various sleazy White House efforts to spy on political opponents. But he offers no evidence at all that ODALE or DEA were designed or led with political spying or a White House power grab as the end in view. Indeed, such evidence as he has either contradicts his conclusions or at best permits him to choose arbitrarily between several competing explanations offered by participants. With respect to the relationship be-

tween the Plumbers and ODALE, the best Epstein can
offer, in notes at the back of his book, is the statement that
the connection between the two "seemed like possibly more
than a simple coincidence" even though "it is not clear to
what extent these converging investigative operations were
planned with a single objective."[41] With respect to the
DEA, Epstein concedes that all those who worked to create
it thought of it as a way of bringing greater efficiency to narcotics law enforcement by reducing organizational rivalries.
Those who lost out in this struggle—the fired head of
BNDD and a Treasury Department official who lost control
over several hundred Customs agents transferred to DEA—
thought of DEA as an effort to create a "national police
force." Epstein weighs this evidence thusly: "I decided that
the quest for power . . . was the dominant purpose" and "I
therefore chose" to characterize the proposal in terms of
power rather than efficiency.[42] In short, the entire "coup
d'état" argument rests on being suspicious about coinci-
dences and a personal (and undefended) decision to believe
the unsupported claims of losers against the explanations of
winners.

It is enough for present purposes, however, to note that
these conflicts raged and that DEA, whatever the motives of
its architects, lacked power and autonomy almost from the
start. Far from being feared as a "national police force,"
DEA was soon under attack in Congress and the administration for being weak and poorly managed. Two years after
DEA was created, the rivalry with Customs was still strong.
In the Office of Management and Budget and in the White
House, the DEA was regarded as a "sick" agency. Management experts in the OMB were skeptical of its budget,
pressed for alterations in its administration, and lacked confidence in its leadership. Justice Department and General
Accounting Office officials demanded that the DEA "measure" its "effectiveness." What the FBI could justify by ideology, salesmanship, and a clean record, the DEA had to jus-

tify by seizures, arrests, the G-DEP system, and "management by objectives." And, of course, it couldn't. One embittered DEA official later complained to an interviewer: "The BNDD-Customs conflict allowed a bunch of self-serving Harvard Business School types to gain power, and our own guys were whores who curried their favor. So we got into a numbers game."

The "Business School types" had, needless to say, a different view of the matter. To them, the BNDD and the DEA were not well managed by even common-sense standards, and the "numbers game" was only a game because the DEA made it so.

Whoever was right, the effect on the agents in the field can be easily imagined. A succession of executives entered office, each announcing a different "priority"—first, identify "trafficking systems"; next, get involved with federal-state-local "task forces" that would make street arrests; then, emphasize dangerous drugs more; next, make cocaine cases; then, stop looking for cocaine and make heroin cases; next, forget about street-level heroin dealers and go after inter-regional, conspiracy-type cases.

Interwoven through the rapid succession of directives was a changing, complex statistical reporting system that had the effect, in most offices, not of generating a desire to succeed by concentrating everything on making big cases, but of creating what one manager later called a "fear of failure" and a need to "make some stats" because that is what the bosses want. As explained in chapter 4, a statistical system intended to help achieve objectives in fact contributed to an attitude that made attaining those objectives more difficult. To that explanation can now be added this further explanation: the fact that there was an elaborate statistical system at all was the result of the weak autonomy of the organization and its great vulnerability to executive and legislative branch critics and rivals. The "rational," objectives-oriented data system of the DEA was the result of weakness; the meaningless,

publicity-oriented data system of the FBI was the product
of strength.

To some in the DEA, the statistics were pure public relations designed to please Congress. As one senior and experienced field administrator told an interviewer, "[My former
boss] taught me what I know—you work one week a month
for Congress and public relations by making the little cases
and the other three weeks for yourself, getting good but
time-consuming cases." In fact, this interpretation missed
the point. Congress, at least in the vital appropriations process, rarely if ever expressed any desire to see many arrests
of small dealers. The House Appropriations Subcommittee,
to judge by the printed record over several years, was no
more "hoodwinked" (in Congressman Rooney's language) by
DEA "stats" than by FBI ones. In fact, the DEA statistics
were used *against* it by congressional committees critical of
the agency—because of integrity lapses, for partisan reasons, or as a result of genuine concern over the drug problem. If Congress made any demands, it was for more big, national or international conspiracy cases whatever the cost in
seizures or arrests.

In a beleaguered agency, the executive spends his time
looking outside. John R. Bartels, Jr., was later to say that he
spent most of his time dealing with outside pressures, especially trying to build support for the DEA (and later to sal-
vage it for himself) within the Department of Justice and in
Congress. His successor, Henry Dogin, was appointed only
on an acting basis and thus he had no long-term concerns; he
was able to devote more time to internal affairs. Peter Bensinger, who followed Dogin, was a man of great energy who
tried, by keeping an exhausting schedule, to deal both with
outside pressures and internal ones.

In such a condition, management obviously will suffer.
Whatever criticisms one may make of the FBI headquarters
staff, it ensured that orders were followed, things got done,
investigations were completed. DEA headquarters was

scarcely the monolith one encountered at the FBI (the best evidence of this was the great willingness of DEA managers compared to FBI ones to air their complaints and repeat their gossip to almost any outsiders who wandered in), but neither was it especially effective in asserting any kind of control over the field.

But nothing is ever completely chaotic—when power slips through the fingers of line managers, it does not simply disappear. It falls instead into the hands of the career administrators who manage the budget, the personnel system, and the purchasing procedures. As an OMB official was later to describe DEA management to an interviewer, "Smith [a pseudonym] has a fiefdom over there." With no one in charge of the program, the person who controls intraagency budget allocations was *de facto* in charge. This is not simply the accident of personality, or the consequence of a nimble ability to get one's hands on the money, but rather the result of managing an organization in an environment in which important constraints on managerial discretion are the legal rules administered by powerful external organizations, such as budget and personnel offices. There are other constraints as well—partisan, clientele, legislative, informational—but these political forces operate directly on the executive. If he masters them, he is powerful; if he does not, his power is dissipated, and another set of constraints, the legal ones, become the source of power. The career administrators are the beneficiaries. One must be very confident to challenge that legalistic power, for whereas an error on a political matter can cost one his job, a false step in the handling of money or personnel appointments can expose one to scandal and even criminal prosecution.

CHAPTER

7

Conclusions

TO A SUBSTANTIAL DEGREE, the administrative systems of the Federal Bureau of Investigation and the Drug Enforcement Administration have been shaped by the political maintenance needs of the two organizations rather than by the nature of the tasks the organizations' operators performed.

For the FBI, its critical problem was to develop public confidence in an agency whose early history was marred by controversy, corruption, partisanship, and incompetence. The administrative system devised by Hoover was brilliantly successful in eliminating the obvious abuses of power and in cultivating favorable public opinion that was readily convertible into strong congressional support. That system had as its object preventing or minimizing misconduct, scandal, and internal bickering and attracting and holding agent personnel who were competent and presentable.

The essential maintenance problem of the DEA, after the drug epidemics of the 1960s had made its tasks both important and controversial, was to cope with a set of bureaucratic rivals (Customs), under circumstances that made it virtually impossible for the agency to show that it was successfully combating the problem of drugs. Unlike the FBI, it could not rely on generalized public support; instead, it was required to produce measures of its own performance, but these measures, by their very nature, seemed to show that the agency was devoting its efforts to relatively low-level, presumably unimportant drug dealers and that it was not always seizing more drugs than its governmental competitors.

In an organizationally ideal world, which is to say in a world free of politics and public opinion, the management systems of the two agencies might have been defined by the nature of the central tasks their operators performed. FBI agents, insofar as they function as detectives, are chiefly concerned with interviewing citizens, developing informants, and recording information. DEA agents are chiefly concerned with inducing criminals to engage under agent surveillance in actions that are illegal or risky. In each case, administrators have an opportunity to affect the way the performance of these tasks serves agency goals in two ways: first, by selecting and training personnel so as to maximize the presence in the organization of the key skills necessary to carry out these tasks and, second, by establishing and enforcing priorities to guide agents in the application of these skills.

But these organizations do not exist in an ideal world, free of constraints. Until recently, the FBI never seriously asked what its investigative priorities were, at least in the criminal field, in part because the Bureau had a strong interest in persuading the public that it investigated *every* violation of federal law over which it had jurisdiction in order to forestall any accusation that it was "selective," and thus possibly partisan, in its choice of cases. Nor has the Bureau until now given even fleeting consideration to the possibility of devising some measure of the success of its investigative efforts. Since it had no bureaucratic rivals, it had no need to demonstrate any relative advantage, and as far as proving its absolute worth it was enough to show that it had a constantly rising workload that produced, year after year, a "record" number of convictions, fines, savings, and recoveries. Its image as a highly centralized, even monolithic agency was, despite periodic criticism from those who disliked Hoover, highly useful, not only to the agency but to the public—it meant that responsibility was clearly fixed, in Hoover himself, for the Bureau's successes and failures. This virtue may have been obscured for many years when it seemed that the FBI had only successes, but once some failures or abuses became evident, there was no doubt in anyone's mind where blame should be placed.

The reality of the Bureau during all this time was somewhat different. Though personnel controls were as highly centralized as it is possible to imagine, the day-to-day investigative work was highly decentralized, with agents having enormous latitude in allocating their time and carrying out their assignments. As it turns out, the nature of the investigative tasks makes their performance necessarily individualized, localized, and of low visibility. Though publicly claiming that its agents were merely parts of a centrally run machine, privately Bureau personnel knew that investigative work had to be left to the agent on the street but took comfort in the fact that the organization's ability to impose swift and severe punishment on any erring agents would induce them to carry out their work with frequent and anxious glances over their shoulder and thus, in all probability, with due regard for the need to be honest and efficient.

The DEA, on the other hand, frequently asks what its priorities are and makes, at the headquarters level, many efforts to state, revise, clarify, and measure them. That it has so little success in making agent behavior conform to headquarters priorities arises from the very structure of the agency. Once the "drug scare" became a national issue, the DEA and the BNDD could no longer be what the FBN once was—a small, elite, national organization devoted to tracking down big smugglers. The BNDD, and the DEA after it, had to be present in every large city and in many small ones. *Every* state acquired a DEA office, and not because a Wyoming or a South Dakota had massive drug problems. Furthermore, the fact that the DEA, like the FBI, shares jurisdiction with state and local police departments means that the federal agency must cultivate the goodwill of, and provide some services to, these departments, in part for political reasons (Congress will not treat kindly any federal agency that ignores "local needs") and in part because federal agencies are to a degree dependent on local ones for investigatory assistance—checking out names, recruiting informants, gathering intelligence. The localistic bias of the DEA and the BNDD was increased by the fact that four successive administrators came from outside narcotics law enforcement and thus were aware they had to prove themselves to the agents. In many cases, this meant deferring to them by, among other things, encouraging the decentralization of the agency and the assumption of power by regional directors.

A drug enforcement agency organized at the street level into investigative squads with local responsibilities will inevitably be dominated by a work ethos that awards status to, and thus emphasizes, making cases—big cases if possible, but cases in any event. Persons who are not agents—not "1811s," in the personnel jargon of the DEA—will not acquire much status or influence, and the work of nonagents will accordingly receive little priority on a day-to-day basis. Thus, personnel assigned to ensure that drug manufacturers comply with federal regulations, investigators who have an interest in amphetamines and barbiturates rather than heroin and cocaine, and intelligence specialists with little or no law enforcement experience will play relatively minor roles in the organization, whatever the announced headquarters policy about the importance of compliance, pills, and intelligence.

These constraints on what an outsider might regard as "rational" administration do not arise because the executives and managers of these agencies are shortsighted, even though (understandably) they may come to accept and even endorse that which they are powerless to alter. The constraints arise instead out of the fact that these are *governmental* agencies, and especially out of the fact that they function in the particular constitutional and political arrangements of American government. The separation of powers between the executive and legislative branches means that no agency can assume that merely because it has the statutory authority to carry out its mission it will have the necessary political support to do so. Every agency must prove its value not only to the cabinet officers who direct it but to a Congress that is not inclined to take executive claims on faith. And if, as is likely to be the case, an agency has bureaucratic rivals that claim a share in its jurisdiction, then the struggle over autonomy must be carried out publicly, before Congress, and before committees and legislators who have their own favorites. That the FBI was able to avoid, for nearly half a century, any serious threats to its autonomy is, in retrospect, quite remarkable. The DEA, with its many competitors, is more nearly the typical case, as the executives of the various military services will glumly testify.

The federal structure of government means that, whatever else an agency does, it has come to terms with the fact that political power in this country is assembled and used chiefly at the local level, if not by local governments then by congressmen and senators who win office by mastering local political conflicts. Agents in both the FBI and the DEA often fail to understand this. They see Congress as a group of officeholders who demand dazzling statistics and public relations gimmicks as a condition for approving budget appropriations. Though there may be some of that, by and large, at least among the knowledgeable legislators serving on the relevant committees, the congressional interest is in whether, and to what extent, a federal agency serves constituent needs that are, if not locally defined, then illustrated by local examples. FBI and DEA budget hearings are not, contrary to agent belief, dominated by a discussion of statistics or performance measures, but by questions about the drug or crime situation in particular localities, the needs of local police departments for aid and cooperation, allegations of misconduct in various communities, and the work of the agency in handling named crimes, extremist activities, and drug-trafficking groups.

This is all the more the case when a government agency is carrying out a task that cannot be fully, and objectively evaluated by any feasible performance measure. In these instances, it is hard to point to substantive results that will outweigh specific errors or misdeeds. FBI administrators never tried to develop a serious performance measure, in part, one may surmise, because they knew it would do no good and in part because such a measure would show that FBI agents, like any investigators, can solve only a small fraction of their cases. Happily for the FBI, it was never under any pressure to produce such a measure. Unhappily for the DEA, it was. What that measure indicated, as stated before, was that the DEA was arresting a lot of low-level drug dealers. That, perhaps, could be explained away—after all, given the way it had organized its task, it was inevitable and perhaps necessary that small dealers be arrested—but no such explanation would be very helpful if the agency had to counter charges of misconduct or corruption. It is a central fact of life for government executives that they are much less likely to be rewarded for their substantive, but hard-to-measure, successes than they are to be penalized for their visible failures. Just as legislators must worry about having to run for reelection against their mistakes, so also must high-level bureaucrats worry about being frustrated or removed by their agency's blunders.

The congressional hearings in which DEA statistics have been most thoroughly scrutinized and criticized have not been the budget hearings conducted by the House Appro-

priations Subcommittee but the Senate hearings conducted
by a subcommittee of the Government Operations Committee that was investigating allegations of misconduct and corruption. The "statistics game" afflicting the DEA has arisen
out of a congressional concern not over effectiveness but
over honesty. Questions about effectiveness were raised in
the context of and as a sideline to an inquiry into integrity.
Though other congressional committees may review the effectiveness of other federal agencies directly—that is, without a prior interest in misconduct—that has not happened in
law enforcement. For four decades, scarcely any congressional questions about FBI effectiveness were asked until
the FBI was charged with political misconduct. The FBI and
the DEA have not experienced serious oversight, but only
feast or famine—invincible when popular, defenseless when
not. That is scarcely the environment in which a reasonable
management system might evolve.

The constraints on the executives of federal investigative
agencies, and their adaptive responses to them, are very
much like the situation in which local police chiefs find
themselves. A chief has little reliable information about the
effect on crime of various patrol techniques or about the performance of individual patrol officers. Thus, although patrol
is the essence of the local police function, relatively few
police administrators devote any effort to planning or analyzing patrol work or to experimentation on the effects of alternative ways of deploying patrol forces. Indeed, many, perhaps most, police chiefs believe that it is risky to do this:
lower-level commanders will be upset, police unions will
complain, and—perhaps worst of all—any visible experiment or plan may fail, leading to adverse political consequences for the department or the chief. Police administration, like federal investigative administration, is chiefly
designed to anticipate and manage the maintenance needs of
the organization. In the case of the police, this means pro-
mulgating and enforcing rules intended to prevent the oc-

currence of that state of affairs most costly to the department—not a rising crime rate, but revelations of corruption,
fiscal malfeasance, and citizen complaints of misconduct.
Thus, police management consists, to a large degree, of mul-
tiplying rules that tell patrol officers what they should *not*
do, rather than what they should do, both to reduce the
chances of their doing something wrong and (equally important) to provide grounds for defending the organization
when something does go wrong ("it's not our fault, he broke
a rule").[1]

Because of the high costs of violating such important governmental constraints as fiscal accountability, financial integrity, proper hiring and personnel policies, and providing information to the public, power in a government agency will
flow, unless there is a strong and successful chief executive,
into the hands of those administrators who enforce government-wide rules within an agency—that is, to the budgetary, personnel, and general administrative officials. The
conventional view that there is an important difference between "line" (i.e., operator) and "staff" units in an organization is, in my opinion, quite correct. One need only over-
hear a few conversations in which line supervisors berate
staff personnel for being "hidebound," "rigid," and "petty"
while staff officers accuse line supervisors of being "power-
hungry," "out of control," or "insensitive" to appreciate the
magnitude of the difference in perspective. But the corollary
of this view—that the staff exists to serve the line—is quite
misleading. In a business firm, where sales are made and
profits earned, perhaps line managers can keep the upper
hand, but in a government agency, with a product that is not
priced on the market and with revenue that is dependent on
political support rather than customer satisfaction, it is the
rare line administrator who can afford to ignore or run
roughshod over the head of the general administrative division. Hoover understood this so well that he made the FBI's
Administrative Division the institutional expression of his

personal control of the Bureau. DEA administrators have learned to their sorrow how costly it can be to suppose that line administrators promoted from the ranks of enforcement agents can easily control their agency's permanent civil service.

If the administrative system of these federal agencies is dominated by the political maintenance needs of the organization, then those needs can best be understood in terms of the desire for autonomy. In chapter 6 the nature of, and the executive's concern for, autonomy was explained; that argument need not be repeated here. This is not to say that administrators walk through the corridors of FBI or DEA headquarters murmuring "autonomy, autonomy" or that there is no consideration of large, substantive concerns. DEA administrators frequently discuss how best to cope with, for example, the problem of heroin imported from Mexico, and FBI officials devote much time to thinking up new ways of combating terrorism or identifying fingerprints. But the dominant concern at the *executive* level, whether or not the executives like it, is with protecting the agency from critics and rivals. Whatever they wanted to accomplish when they took office, it is not long before they come to see their day as dominated by the need to react to the environment and to view that environment as composed of real and potential threats.

Those who think government agencies are by nature imperialistic and expansionist simply do not understand the situation. Neither Hoover nor his successors, nor any of the executives of the DEA, spent much time trying to make their agencies bigger—they spent their time trying to make them more secure. Occasionally this meant reaching out for new powers or attacking a rival, but typically this was to achieve more defensible organizational boundaries. Naturally, every executive thinks he requires more funds, and both the FBI and the DEA were notably successful in getting them, but it was not its budget that made the FBI so formidable or the DEA so weak.

Within the organization, the same struggle for autonomy occurs, but at the level of divisions, offices, units, and squads. When change is proposed from above, it is evaluated by the managers of these suborganizations in terms of whether it will enhance or reduce the unit's autonomy. SACs in the FBI resisted the quality case program because they feared it would cost them resources. The planners in the Office of Planning and Evaluation were seen as unrealistic or even threatening when they proposed new statistical measures of performance or new formulas for allocating personnel among field offices. Regional directors in the DEA often bristled at headquarters directives about the emphasis that should be given to heroin, cocaine, or dangerous drugs, or to the needs for interregional conspiracy cases. In both the FBI and the DEA, this resistance did not flow from any opposition to the goals of the organization or to the purposes of the directives but rather from the belief that headquarters "doesn't understand what it's like in the field" and the fear that new measures, policies, and formulas would lead to one's own field office losing personnel and funds when it is evident from conditions on the street that the office already lacks enough resources to do its job properly.

Headquarters administrators usually understand this fear, but they have very few incentives at their disposal with which to overcome it. They cannot easily affect the pay or rank of a recalcitrant field administrator; those things are determined by Congress and the Civil Service Commission. They can consider transferring him, but there is a limit to how much that will help—the new appointee is likely to acquire the same point of view as his predecessor, and transfers cannot go on endlessly. Nor can they always threaten to deny him promotion: a SAC or regional director is already near the top, and end, of his career. Thus, headquarters must try to make changes either by developing a pattern of rule so autocratic that no one will dare challenge it (as with Hoover) or it must proceed by persuasion, consultation, or indirection (as with Hoover's successors and all DEA administrators). Furthermore, field administrators are likely to have strong ties to local authorities including, possibly, governors, congressmen, and police chiefs, and these alliances are disrupted only at the executive's peril.

Again, the success of Hoover in overcoming these constraints on change was remarkable. He was strong enough to resist for many years FBI involvement in organized crime and civil rights cases, but when the time came, in his eyes, to change, he was also strong enough to make the organization change with him. At one time, Hoover asserted that "no single individual or coalition of racketeers dominates organized crime across the nation"[2]—in short, the Mafia is a myth. Then a New York state police trooper in 1957 stumbled across the Apalachin meeting of dozens of top gangland figures from across the country and the Justice Department, first under President Eisenhower and then, on a larger scale, under President Kennedy, created an Organized Crime unit among its attorneys. After the FBI had eavesdropped on some gangland meetings and acquired a few highly placed informants, Hoover moved swiftly to ensure that each field office would give serious attention to organized crime by creating special squads for its investigation. Suddenly, the Mafia existed—or more accurately, "LCN" (La Cosa Nostra) existed.

It is easy to be amused by this switch, but one also has to be impressed by it. In retrospect, it seems clear that many of the things the FBI did that, when revealed, aroused public criticism represented the defects of the Bureau's organizational virtues. An organization strong enough to stamp out agent corruption and partisanship, to resist presidential directives regarding domestic counterintelligence, to insist that the civil liberties of suspects be protected long before the Supreme Court required it, and to investigate the Ku Klux Klan even when it had many powerful political allies was also strong enough to launch an investigation of domestic radicals without any guidelines, to serve the partisan interests of various presidents who wanted to know things about their political rivals, and to attempt to discredit groups that had broken no laws. Now that Hoover's successors have decided to put more authority in the hands of field administrators and allow for the development of different law enforcement priorities in different communities, the Bureau discovers that, though this change is slow and difficult, it is much easier to decentralize something that has first been centralized.

The disjunction between tasks and administration and the concern for autonomy so evident in the FBI and the DEA may not occur to the same degree in other government agencies. Different tasks performed in different political circumstances may lend themselves more readily to effective management. I conjecture that there are three prerequisites for the rational adaptation of management to tasks in an organization. First, the goals must be sufficiently operational so that one can make a reasonably unambiguous judgment as to whether the desired state of affairs has actually been brought into being. Some agencies have such goals—the National Aeronautics and Space Administration could tell when it had placed a man on the moon. Many—probably most—government agencies do not have such goals: what is an educated child, a good foreign policy, a well-managed forest?

Second, the organization must have the technology to achieve its goal. The Bureau of Public Roads knows how to build highways, but the Bureau of Prisons does not know how to rehabilitate a criminal, nor does the National Institute of Drug Abuse know how to cure a heroin addict.

Third, the organization must be reasonably free to apply a suitable technology to a given objective. There are only rather mild restrictions on the freedom of the Census Bureau to count citizens or on a fire department to put out fires. There are pervasive and complex constraints on the freedom of the Postal Service to open or close post offices or to hire and fire letter carriers.

Where a government agency is created to serve a goal that is ambiguously and equivocally stated, when it has an uncertain or inadequate technology at its disposal, and when political expectations about how its services should be distributed or conducted are sharp and numerous, the agency has only the slimmest chance of allowing its management system to be shaped by its tasks. No doubt there are government agencies that can be found at every point on the continuum described by these three factors, but I think it reasonable to believe that most are at the hard-to-manage end. After all, we turn to government in part precisely *because* we wish to attain vague, complex, controversial, hard-to-produce objectives (clear, easily attained, noncontroversial goals are more often than not left to the market or to private arrangements). And all government agencies must accept to some degree the constraints of being in the public sector, and many, because of our sensitivities as to what is right and proper (or self-serving), are especially vulnerable to them.

In short, though there is no reason to believe that the management problems of the FBI and the DEA are identical to those in all other public enterprises, there is also little reason to suppose that they are unique. Many, perhaps most, government agencies, because of their tasks and their political environment, display management methods and maintenance strategies that are not *task oriented* but instead *constraint oriented.*

Without altering the Constitution, eliminating the force of public opinion, and seeking only obtainable goals, little can be done to change a constraint-oriented bureau into one that is task oriented. But that does not mean that management cannot be made better, at least at the margin. Constraints do not uniquely determine how administrators shall behave, they only reduce significantly the room to maneuver. If one wishes to think practically about the matter, the place to begin is with the process by which the central tasks of the agency are defined. In organizations with vague goals or inadequate technologies, tasks are shaped by features of the situation that are tangential to, or independent of, stated goals. These features are chiefly three: the personal predilections and professional experiences of the operators, the formal and informal reward system of the organization, and the imperatives of the situation with which the operator must regularly cope.

This study sheds no light on whether the personality or social background of agents importantly affects the way they define their tasks. In my opinion, there is little reason to believe that such factors have more than a marginal importance. They may, of course, influence how well an agent does his work and how favorably he is viewed by the public, but it is hard to imagine that the nature of the job itself would be different if different kinds of men and women were hired.[3] The prior experience of the agents on the job, however, does affect their work. DEA agents were, in large measure, once BNDD agents, and many of these—and most of the key supervisors—were before that FBN agents. For several decades, those organizations have trained and deployed persons to do undercover work. FBI agents have for decades acquired experience at cultivating informants and interviewing citizens.

It would be remarkable if the formative experiences of one generation of agents did not provide the examples and cues for a new generation of agents. The better agents often become managers and thus acquire the power as well as the opportunity to shape incoming agents. And a "better" agent—and thus an influential agent—is often precisely the one who most fully exemplifies and takes pride in the traditions of the organization.

The formal reward system of the organization reinforces or penalizes particular behavior. FBI rules once required agents to carry a certain number of cases, to post those cases, and to accumulate certain "statistical accomplishments"; DEA rules were perceived as requiring a certain number of arrests and seizures. The informal reward system has been much more important, perhaps because in these organizations, unlike others in which tasks are more easily placed under continuous administration scrutiny, much of what an agent does on the street is known only to his colleagues. In the FBI, good agents are those who make "big cases" and who develop important informants; in the DEA, good agents are those who are street-wise, can produce big undercover buys, and who have good snitches. In both agencies, but especially in the FBI, there has been some tension between the formal and informal reward systems. FBI agents felt they had to "make stats" at the expense of working big cases and could only be promoted by seeking "administrative advancement" through skill in "paper-shuffling." DEA agents believed, rightly or wrongly, that quantity counted more than quality, though in part this was because living up to the expectations of their colleagues often meant proving they could work the street.

The imperatives of the situation include all those elements of the operator's environment with which he must cope successfully if he is to achieve any results or even survive. Often this coping is at odds with what the organization claims to be doing. Whatever the announced purposes of prisons, prison guards must first and foremost devise ways of protecting themselves against inmate violence, and thus they will emphasize security over rehabilitation, deterrence, justice, or whatever else those in authority say is important.[4] Police patrol officers must handle disputes and disorderly behavior whether or not the law is broken or an arrest can be made.[5] Investigators must extract reliable information from citizens, many of whom are fearful, suspicious, conniving, guilty, eccentric, or untruthful. FBI agents spend more time with law-abiding citizens than with guilty ones, and thus they need to convey an image of respectability, confidence, and trustworthiness more than DEA agents, for whom the opposite appearance is generally more useful. The former only rarely need to fear violence; the latter must be prepared for it at all times.

If an organization such as the FBI or the DEA wishes to change how its tasks are defined or the ways in which its operators behave, it must try to alter the traditions of the operators, the informal reward systems of the working groups, or the imperatives of the situation. To change any of these factors requires Herculean efforts of the sort that are not likely to issue from headquarters directives or in-service training programs. The very core of the organization must be torn apart and rebuilt. Suppose, for example, that DEA administrators wanted to see their agency devote more of its efforts to gathering intelligence about high-level traffickers. Piecemeal efforts to achieve this will almost surely fail. Assigning intelligence specialists to work alongside instigator agents will lead to either conflict between utterly different operating styles or to one set of operators—those who share in the organization's strongest traditions—ignoring or dominating those that do not. Telling existing instigators to stop working undercover and to start working on intelligence matters is to cause them to lose status in the eyes of their colleagues and to operate in the face of hostile peer-group pressure. Instead, one would have to hire new operators and set them to work in their own environment with supervisors able and willing to build new dominant traditions and organizational ideologies.

If one wished to make the DEA a conspiracy-indicting rather than informant-recruiting agency, one would have to replace many of its operators and administrators with new personnel charged with wholly new tasks. One might, for example, hire lawyers, organize them into task forces directed at particular underworld organizations, and put their management in the hands of higher-ranking lawyers. (That is, of course, exactly what is done with organized crime strike forces.) That would change the DEA fundamentally—indeed, it would become an entirely different organization.

Such an organization would have many advantages, but it would have one disadvantage—it would not generate out of its own resources significant numbers of case leads. It would have to obtain its informants from some other agency. That "other agency," if it existed at all, would, of course, look very much like the DEA.

So long as the central task remains unchanged, however, the imperatives of the situation facing those who must perform that task will reinforce a way of operating that organizational administrators will find it hard to change. If there is to be criminal and narcotics investigation, those who do it will have to cope with what FBI and DEA agents now confront. This is well understood in the organizations but not outside them. Some citizens are dismayed by the fact that narcotics agents make undercover buys. Though the amount of such buying can, within limits, be altered, the alternative to behaving in this way is to make, *de facto*, the sale of narcotics legal. There is no third choice. Similarly, some citizens recoil at the thought of investigators recruiting and manipulating informants and wish to see this practice reduced or severely curtailed. That is tantamount to abandoning criminal investigation, though not to arresting criminals. Many arrests will continue to be made and many cases will go on being solved by patrol officers who catch people red-handed or who get reliable information from victims or witnesses. But where cases cannot be solved in this way, investigation becomes necessary, and, overwhelmingly, investigation means informants.[6]

Short of the wholesale redefinition of tasks and the replacement of personnel, some marginal but perhaps significant changes might result from altering the reward system of the existing organization. The formal reward system can be examined to see if it is encouraging useless behavior. Where the tasks are difficult to describe statistically, as investigative tasks necessarily are, statistics should be used sparingly to reduce the possibility that agents will emphasize that which is merely measurable. The government-wide enthusiasm for "management by objectives" can lead to the same absurdities as some of Hoover's "statistical accomplishments." If an agency "plans" to allocate 20 percent of agent time to "white-collar" crime or to major heroin traffickers or "plans" to indict one hundred organized crime figures or fifteen operators of clandestine laboratories, the plans will be at best meaningless and at worst perverse. To count informants means to stimulate the accumulation of countable, but probably not productive, informants. To count drug arrests tends to encourage the belief that arrests are important, even if the agency classifies the arrests by type of violator. Obviously, every agency must collect some quantitative data on its performance. Deciding what to collect requires careful executive judgment, for what is at stake is not simply "finding out whether we are attaining our goals" but rather "telling agents what we think is important."

The informal reward system is harder to change to produce the intended effect. Such opportunities as exist for doing so are largely to be found at the level of the primary working group—the squad or its equivalent—in the field office. How squads are organized and what mission they are assigned make a difference. If the director of the FBI instructs the field to give a high priority to "white-collar" and organized crime, little happens, or, more accurately, misleading things happen. When the SAC in charge of a field office creates a new organizational structure in which squads are targeted on "white-collar" and organized crime and relieved of the necessity (or deprived of the possibility) of responding to citizen-initiated crime reports, many things happen. Agents now expect each other to *find* cases rather than *handle* cases; those who do not find any lose status.

If the DEA desires to emphasize high-level conspiracy cases without reconstituting itself fundamentally, it is probably necessary to take agent squads off the street. On the street, they will reward each other on the basis of busts; off the street, they will have to base their mutual esteem on success at analyzing telephone toll slips, sitting on wiretaps, or assembling intelligence. This, of course, was what the CENTAC effort in the DEA was all about, but the agency was administratively too weak to defend that strategy in face of opposition from regional directors. This means that, if making high-level conspiracy cases is the goal, the DEA executive will have to rethink the very structure of his agency and the extent to which he wishes to have regional and district offices at all. That, in turn, requires him to consider the extent to which his agents can perform domestically the same function they now perform internationally—serving as intelligence liaison officers at local police agencies to which they supply information and assistance in exchange for access to informants. I argue here neither for nor against such a plan; everything depends on the importance one attaches to regional and national conspiracy cases. But *if* that is the goal, a localistic agency structure inevitably works against it in ways that cannot be overcome by headquarters directives that "state priorities" (or, in the current bureaucratic jargon, "prioritize the tasks").

The focus on reward systems at the primary working-group level suggests, obviously, the importance of first-line supervisors. Squad supervisors in the FBI and the DEA are perhaps the most neglected link in the administrative system, yet they are clearly the most important. In both agencies, administrative requirements as well as some personal inclinations take these supervisors off the street. Agents complain about this and respect those few supervisors who "hit the bricks." Certainly in the FBI and to some extent in the DEA, the practical function of the squad supervisor is to serve as a clearinghouse for the vast flow of paperwork up and down the hierarchy. All are, of course, expected to evaluate their agents, but the conventional evaluation form leads to perfunctory comments and uniform grades of "very good" or "outstanding." The actual evaluation, or so agents believe, is statistical and done by headquarters. So long as this belief persists, a supervisor's real impact will depend on whether, by chance, he happens to take a constructive interest in the work of his agents. Evaluation of the supervisors, in turn, tends to be based on their suitability for promotion to higher posts, which means, in no small part, on whether they have acquired a "headquarters perspective." Evaluating them *as supervisors,* and rewarding them on that basis, is somewhat hit or miss.

I cannot say, on the basis of this study, that this perspective on organizational management and change is generally applicable. No doubt there are task-oriented agencies that have a very different system of administration. But whatever the recommendations, *the analysis must begin with the tasks.* There is no substitute for knowing the facts at the street level. Unfortunately, this is not how reorganization decisions are usually made in government. Agencies are changed on the basis of a top-down perspective on their problems, and these problems are usually perceived to be ones of "leadership," or its lack, and of headquarters administration. Often such problems arise because of a scandal, or charges of "wasteful duplication," or a congressional investigation of an agency's failure to attain its goals. The proposed remedies typically call for merger, reshuffling, and restructuring—principally in Washington.

It has been proposed, for example, that the FBI and the DEA merge. Presumably the strengths of the FBI—a strong personnel system, a freedom from agent corruption, and a record of making big cases—will offset the alleged weaknesses of the DEA—a decentralized system, frequent charges of corruption or misconduct, and a "buy-and-bust" mentality. My analysis leads me to be suspicious of that argument. Perhaps—no one can know without trying—a merger makes sense. I do not wish here to make a case either for or against the proposal. I wish only to induce the reader to view this idea, and all similar ideas, through the perspective developed in this study. That can be done by learning to ask questions such as the following:

Do the operators of the two organizations perform similar or compatible tasks? (In this case, can one organization have agents who try both to inspire citizen confidence by their upright and conventional demeanor and to deceive criminals by their clever and "hip" manner?)

Do the operators utilize similar resources in similar ways? (In this case, can the FBI policy of never burning an informant be reconciled with the DEA policy of inducing its informants to testify in court? If one agency changes its informant policy to accord with that of the other, what will be the net gain or loss in information?)

Can an administrative system that achieves conformity to important public objectives for one set of operators also guarantee that conformity for another set? (In this case, can an FBI administration that has been successful in preventing agent corruption and ensuring compliance with the search and seizure rules of the Supreme Court achieve the same success when it must deal with narcotics agents who necessarily face great risks of corruption and who must skirt the edges of the rules governing entrapment and illegal searches?)

Will the organizational maintenance strategy of one agency prove compatible with, or as useful for, another agency? (In this case, will the FBI policy of insisting on a monopoly position in its investigations be of any value in a field, such as narcotics enforcement, that places a high premium on cooperative efforts among several rival federal agencies—Customs, Immigration, DEA—as well as a variety of local, state, and foreign police departments?)[7]

A familiarity with tasks, and the resources essential to the performance of those tasks, is also necessary if one wishes to alter the targets of FBI investigations. If we want the Bureau to emphasize "white-collar" and political corruption cases at the expense of domestic security cases, we can achieve that change, as the recent history of the Bureau has shown, but we cannot make that change and at the same time tightly restrict agent use of informants. Most collective and consensual crimes, as defined in chapter 5, as well as many extortionate crimes, provide few opportunities for the Bureau to rely on victim complaints. To become aware of the existence of such offenses, investigations must be to a large degree proactive rather than reactive and must precede the availability of information that would constitute probable cause for making an arrest. In general, such investigations depend on informants, and while some may appear spontaneously—as when a disaffected or fearful member of a political corruption ring walks in off the street and acquaints agents with the existence of the crime—not enough will appear without special efforts at recruitment and inducement to make possible a substantial increase in the number of such cases. It is easy to be critical of some domestic security investigations and to be enthusiastic about more investigations of collective and extortionate crimes, but the problems of defining proper investigative methods are quite similar, and quite difficult to resolve, in each case.

I have argued that the management of investigative tasks has been powerfully shaped by the political maintenance needs of these organizations—that many managers, and all executives, must spend much of their time and energy looking upward and outward rather than downward and inward. That will be seen by many readers as a defect of these agencies. And from the point of view of "rational" administration, it is a defect. But these constraints also have the virtues of their defects: law enforcement in this country is highly sensitive to the wants of political superiors and ultimately to the demands of public opinion.

Excessive zeal in conforming to political demands has led the FBI to undertake some inquiries that had only partisan justification, and a preoccupation with maintaining public support has led it and the DEA to exaggerate their statistical accomplishments and to stimulate public concern over crime, subversion, and drug trafficking. But the same sensitivity to the political environment has also meant that, broadly speaking, these agencies have done what the public wanted done. When crime was on the increase, the FBI went after criminals; when public concern over threats to domestic security was at its peak, the FBI investigated subversives, broadly defined. The Bureau's gradual involvement in civil rights cases paralleled rather closely the gradual shift in public sentiment on the issue of black rights—from a concern over violence perpetrated by the Ku Klux Klan, it steadily moved toward an interest in voting rights and then on to a wider range of citizenship issues. The FBI resisted investigating organized crime until it became clear that the public took the problem seriously; then it moved in vigorously. "White-collar" crime has become an investigative priority in recent years, not because of autonomous decisions within the Bureau, but because of mounting political and public concern.

Much the same has been true of the DEA. It abandoned the flamboyant preoccupation of Harry Anslinger with marijuana cases as public opinion about the seriousness of that drug changed. It intensified its efforts directed at the heroin traffic in the 1960s because public concern over heroin was rising; whatever one believes about the efforts of various politicians to capitalize on it, that worry was a real one for the great majority of citizens. For a time, public hostility toward cocaine seemed as strong and united as its antipathy to heroin; thus, DEA agents made many cocaine cases. No sooner did some segments of medical and public opinion begin to question whether cocaine belonged in the same category as heroin than DEA agents were told to make certain they were not overemphasizing cocaine cases.

The conformity of investigative priorities and public opinion is not exact because public opinion is itself divided on some questions and not accurately represented in the

Congress or the media on others. And the zeal of some legislators to find whipping boys with which to advance their views or ambitions can lead to a harmful overreaction to past abuses. What once was left, unwisely, entirely to agency discretion when the FBI or the FBN enjoyed unchallenged popular support is in danger, just as unwisely, of being made subject to the most detailed legislative and administrative regulation now that both agencies are on the defensive. In time, one suspects, a reasonable balance will be struck.

Some readers will be amused or dismayed by the consequences of attempting to manage investigative organizations in a political environment that makes organizational maintenance so difficult. They should pause and reflect on what such agencies might be like, and thus what their feelings would be, if a powerful law enforcement organization were free to design and operate its administrative system solely, or even chiefly, on the basis of what the agents' task required. Such organizations exist in the world, perhaps in most nations of the world, and their record, judged by the test of human liberty, is not promising.

Review acclaim for *Thinking About Crime*

by James Q. Wilson

"... is America's leading academic authority on crime. He has served on important commissions, advised presidents and written a very good book about police. He is an academic who is not ashamed to write sentences ordinary folk can take pleasure in reading. He is an unconventional thinker. He was studying the police and crime in the early 1960s, when the subject was as fashionable at Harvard as dog racing." —*The Washington Post*

"... is animated by a spirit of justice and, much like Learned Hand, by a spirit of liberty. He will attempt to understand what can be accomplished by government in an open, nontotalitarian society, and he will appreciate whatever progress is achieved. Such a view requires an understanding of both the abilities of government and its limitations. A rare understanding these days." —*The Alternative*

"Here is wisdom, clarity of language, thoughtful alternatives for public policy and broad erudition.... Wilson's style of writing deserves special note, not simply because he writes well, clearly and with measured parsimony; he also has the cautious conditional and subjunctive language of science where assertions are made in the absence of definitive conclusions." —Marvin E. Wolfgang, *The New York Times*

NOTES

Preface

1. During 1972–73, I was chairman of the National Advisory Council for Drug Abuse Prevention, a statutory agency charged with advising the executives of the federal drug enforcement and drug treatment programs. Subsequently, I was a consultant to the administrator of the DEA with responsibility for advising him on a number of management issues, especially those connected with the creation of a policy-planning staff. Still later I was unofficially an adviser to Clarence Kelley, then director of the FBI. This book is not an account of these experiences, nor is it an effort to justify such advice as I might have given. It is, to the best of my ability, an account of how these organizations work, informed in part by my first-hand experience with them but drawing primarily on subsequent research and interviewing.

Chapter 1

1. Two important academic studies of the domestic security and intelligence work of the FBI have recently been completed, both emphasizing the relationship between security investigations and constitutional issues: Richard E. Morgan, *Domestic Intelligence: Monitoring Dissent in America* (New York: Twentieth Century Fund, forthcoming) and John T. Elliff, *The Reform of FBI Intelligence* (tentative title) (Washington, D.C.: Police Foundation, forthcoming).

2. A bureaucracy is a special kind of organization. By organization, I mean (following Barnard) a consciously coordinated system of activities among two or more persons. A bureaucracy is a large organization in which the responsibility for achieving this coordination is divided among several appointed officials. Where one person—the executive or leader—can unaided achieve the requisite level of coordinated behavior, bureaucracy does not exist. Where one person cannot (or, I suppose, will not) accomplish this alone, subordinate officials share in the task, creating the problem of coordinating the coordinators—the central problem of large-scale bureaucratic structures.

3. Chester I. Barnard, *The Functions of the Executive* (Cambridge, Mass.: Harvard University Press, 1938), p. 217.

4. Philip Selznick, *Leadership in Administration* (Evanston, Ill.: Row, Peterson & Co., 1957), pp. 17, 42–56.

5. Henri Fayol, *General and Industrial Management* (London: Pitman, 1949) and the papers by Fayol and by Gulick and Urwick in Luther Gulick and Lyndall Urwick, eds., *Papers on the Science of Administration* (New York: Institute of Public Administration, 1937).

6. Herbert A. Simon, *Administrative Behavior*, 2d ed. (New York: Macmillan, 1959), chaps. 2–4.

7. Richard M. Cyert and James G. March, *A Behavioral Theory of the Firm* (Englewood Cliffs, N.J.: Prentice-Hall, 1963), chap. 6.

8. James D. Thompson, *Organizations in Action* (New York: McGraw-Hill, 1967).

9. Frank S. Levy, Arnold J. Meltsner, and Aaron Wildavsky, *Urban Outcomes* (Berkeley: University of California Press, 1974), chap. 4.

10. Herbert Kaufman, *The Forest Ranger* (Baltimore: Johns Hopkins Press, 1960).

11. James Q. Wilson, *Varieties of Police Behavior* (Cambridge, Mass.: Harvard University Press, 1968); William Ker Muir, Jr., *Police: Streetcorner Politicians* (Chicago: University of Chicago Press, 1977); Jonathan Rubinstein, *City Police* (New York: Farrar, Straus, & Giroux, 1973).

12. Gresham M. Sykes, *The Society of Captives* (Princeton, N.J.: Princeton University Press, 1958).

13. Donald P. Warwick, *A Theory of Public Bureaucracy: Politics, Personality, and Organization in the State Department* (Cambridge, Mass.: Harvard University Press, 1975); William I. Bacchus, *Foreign Policy and the Bureaucratic Process* (Princeton, N.J.: Princeton University Press, 1974).

14. Peter M. Blau, *The Dynamics of Bureaucracy* (Chicago: University of Chicago Press, 1955).

15. Selznick, *Leadership in Administration*, and Morton H. Halperin, *Bureaucratic Politics and Foreign Policy* (Washington, D.C.: Brookings Institution, 1974).

16. Selznick, *Leadership in Administration*, p. 66.

17. Paul R. Lawrence and Jay W. Lorsch, *Organization and Environment* (Boston: Graduate School of Business, Harvard University, 1967).

Chapter 2

1. Peter W. Greenwood et al., *The Criminal Investigation Process*, vol. 3, *Observations and Analysis* (Santa Monica: RAND, 1975), pp. 67, 70.

2. From an unpublished study by the Police Foundation, Washington, D.C.

3. James Q. Wilson, *Varieties of Police Behavior* (Cambridge, Mass.: Harvard University Press, 1968), p. 16.

4. This total excludes supervisors, agents with noninvestigative duties, and agents assigned to Resident Agencies.

5. Jerome H. Skolnick, *Justice Without Trial* (New York: John Wiley, 1966), pp. 42–48; Wilson, *Varieties of Police Behavior*, pp. 19–20.

6. Federal Bureau of Investigation, *Uniform Crime Reports, 1974* (Washington: Government Printing Office, 1974), pp. 223–27.

7. *United States Code*, Title 18, sec. 2312.

8. This policy was adopted by the Department of Justice on June 1, 1970, and made part of the manual given to United States attorneys.

9. *United States Code*, Title 18, sec. 2314.

10. *United States Code*, Title 18, sec. 659.

11. Sanford J. Ungar, *FBI* (Boston: Atlantic Monthly Press-Little, Brown & Co., 1976), p. 406.

12. From data kindly supplied to the author by the director of the Administrative Office of the United States Courts, Washington, D.C.

13. Michael J. Hindelang et al., eds., *Sourcebook of Criminal Justice Statistics, 1974* (Washington, D.C.: U.S. Department of Justice, National Criminal Justice Information and Statistics Service, 1975), p. 482.

14. Cf. Mark H. Moore, *Buy and Bust* (Lexington, Mass.: Lexington Books, 1977), chap. 3.

15. Moore, *Buy and Bust*, chap. 4.

16. *United States Code*, Title 21, sec. 844.

17. Drug Enforcement Administration, "Drug Enforcement Statistical Report" (December 1975).

18. Drug Enforcement Administration, "Mission Statement" (April 9, 1976). Emphasis added.

19. *United States Code*, Title 19, sec. 841.

20. *United States Code*, Title 21, sec. 846.

21. *United States Code*, Title 18, secs. 2516, 2518.

22. Classified in accordance with the Comprehensive Drug Abuse Prevention and Control Act of 1970, *United States Code*, Title 21, secs. 801–966.

23. Drug Enforcement Administration, "Drug Enforcement Statistical Report" (September 1975).

Chapter 3

1. Robert Daley, "Inside the Criminal-Informant Business," *New York Magazine* (March 24, 1975), pp. 31–35.

2. See, for example, the account of the infiltration of the Socialist Workers' Party by Timothy Redfearn in *New York Times*, August 2, 1976.

3. Informants are assigned to one of three categories: criminal, organized crime, and domestic security.

4. Hoffa v. U.S., 385 US 293 (1966).

5. On Lee v. U.S., 343 US 747 (1952); Lopez v. U.S., 373 US 427 (1963).

6. Rovario v. U.S., 353 US 53 (1957).

7. Ibid.

8. 386 US 300 (1967).

9. Smith v. Illinois, 390 US 129 (1968).

10. Shore v. U.S., 49 F2d 519 (1931); U.S. v. Hanna, 341 F2d 906 (1965); Sorrentino v. U.S., 163 F2d 627 (1947).

11. Portomene v. U.S., 221 F2d 582 (1955); U.S. v. Lamar, 337 F2d 349 (1964); U.S. v. Conforti, 200 F2d 365 (1952); White v. U.S., 330 F2d 811 (1964).

12. See, for example, the rulings of the New York Court of Appeals in People v. Coggins and People v. Brown, 34 N.Y. 2d 163 (1974). The reader should also bear in mind that for the police to make, with or without the aid of an informant, an undercover purchase of illegal goods does not, by itself, constitute a violation of the suspect's right to be free of entrapment so long as the suspect was ready and willing to commit the crime and was awaiting any propitious opportunity to do so. The leading opinion is that of Learned Hand in U.S. v. Sherman, 200 F2d 880 (1952).

13. Sanford J. Ungar, *FBI* (Boston: Atlantic Monthly Press-Little, Brown & Co., 1976), p. 450.

14. Daley, "Inside the Criminal-Informant Business," pp. 31–35.

15. Comptroller General of the United States, *FBI Domestic Intelligence*

Operations—Their Purpose and Scope, a report to the House Committee on the Judiciary (Washington, D.C.: General Accounting Office, February 24, 1976), p. 131.

16. Ibid., p. 97.

17. Ibid., p. 47.

18. Ibid., p. 135; see also U.S. Congress, Senate Select Committee to Study Governmental Operations with Respect to Intelligence Activities, *Hearings: Federal Bureau of Investigation,* 94th Cong., 1st sess., 1975, vol. 6, p. 109.

19. Ibid., pp. 110–23.

20. Ibid., p. 122.

21. Ibid., pp. 115–32.

22. Ibid., p. 117.

23. Ibid., p. 118.

24. *United States Code,* Title 18, sec. 4.

25. Memorandum dated December 15, 1976, from Attorney General Edward H. Levi to FBI Director Clarence M. Kelley: "Use of Informants in Domestic Security, Organized Crime, and Other Criminal Investigations."

26. Comptroller General, *FBI Domestic Intelligence Operations,* pp. 108–11.

27. Senate Select Committee, *Hearings,* pp. 370–71.

28. Comptroller General, *FBI Domestic Intelligence Operations,* p. 138.

29. See, for example, the testimony of former attorney general Nicholas Katzenbach in Senate Select Committee, *Hearings,* pp. 198–216, and a memorandum from the Federal Bureau of Investigation to the Senate Select Committee dated January 12, 1976, reprinted in the *Hearings* on pp. 992–1000.

30. Comptroller General of the United States, *FBI Domestic Intelligence Operations: An Uncertain Future,* draft report to the Subcommittee on Civil and Constitutional Rights, House Committee on the Judiciary (November 8, 1977), p. 5.

31. Edward Jay Epstein, *Agency of Fear* (New York: G. P. Putnam's Sons, 1977), pp. 103–10.

32. Ibid., pp. 118, 199, 208–15.

Chapter 4

1. Leonard D. White, *Introduction to the Study of Public Administration,* 4th ed. (New York: Macmillan, 1955), p. 1. Emphasis in original.

2. Herbert A. Simon, *Administrative Behavior,* 2d ed. (New York: Macmillan, 1959), p. 61.

3. Peter M. Blau, *The Dynamics of Bureaucracy* (Chicago: University of Chicago Press, 1955), chaps. 3, 11.

4. Herbert Kaufman, *The Forest Ranger* (Baltimore: Johns Hopkins Press, 1960), chaps. 4, 5.

5. Sanford J. Ungar, *FBI* (Boston: Atlantic Monthly Press-Little, Brown & Co., 1976), p. 95.

6. Federal Bureau of Investigation, *Uniform Crime Reports, 1974,* (Washington, D.C.: Government Printing Office, 1975), p. 42.

7. Jerome H. Skolnick, *Justice Without Trial* (New York: John Wiley, 1966), pp. 167–81.

8. Peter B. Bloch and Cyrus Ulberg, *Auditing Clearance Rates* (Washington, D.C.: Police Foundation, 1974).

9. "Bait money" is funds kept in bank teller drawers that, when removed by a robber, trigger a silent alarm and sometimes in addition emit a powerful dye or smoke.

10.   Cf. Ungar, *FBI*, p. 95; Ovid Demaris, *The Director: An Oral Biography of J. Edgar Hoover* (New York: Harper's Magazine Press, 1975); Joseph L. Schott, *No Left Turns* (New York: Ballantine Books, 1975). Because of the nature of Hoover's relations with the press, the best stories are found principally in books written by his critics. A sympathetic biographer could no doubt produce even more.

11.   Max Weber, *Economy and Society*, vol. 3, ed. Guenther Roth and Claus Wittich (New York: Bedminster Press, 1968), pp. 1006–7.

12.   U.S. Congress, Senate Government Operations Committee, Permanent Subcommittee on Investigations, *Federal Drug Enforcement: Hearings*, 94th Cong., 2d sess., 1975, part 1, p. 100. Hereafter, *Hearings*.

13.   Memorandum from Peter B. Bensinger, administrator of Drug Enforcement Administration, entitled "The DEA Strategy," April 9, 1976.

14.   *Hearings*, Part 1, p. 49.

15.   Ibid.

16.   Ibid., p. 54.

17.   Drug Enforcement Administration, "Report of the Management Task Force to the Acting Administrator and Deputy Administrator" (October 10, 1975), p. 109.

18.   Ibid., p. 112.

19.   Ibid.

20.   Drug Enforcement Administration, "Geo-Drug Enforcement Program: First Year Assessment, Fiscal Year 1974."

21.   Unpublished DEA data made available to author.

22.   Administrative Office of the United States Courts, *Annual Report of the Director*, 1975, Tables D-4, D-5.

23.   Memorandum from the Director of the FBI to all SACs dated June 17, 1975 (file number 62-116423).

Chapter 5

1.   The FBI survey and the subsequent development of the quality case program had complex origins. Headquarters was interviewing local United States attorneys about prosecutive guidelines when it discovered the high proportion of cases in which prosecution was declined. Director Clarence Kelley instructed his staff to look more closely at the problem. At about the same time, I submitted a memorandum to Kelley suggesting the establishment of investigative priorities in place of the emphasis on statistical accomplishments. In all likelihood, the political criticism then being directed at the Bureau made a reevaluation of internal procedures seem a plausible idea. The reader should be aware, however, that I was a sometime participant in the events described in this section. My memorandum was dated May 29, 1974; on June 11, Kelley had lunch with a group of younger Bureau supervisors to hear their concerns; on June 13, he instructed the OPE to begin a study of the use of personnel; the OPE made its initial report to him on August 15. The way in which Kelley broached the issue was an indication of the way FBI Headquarters thought of caseloads at the time. He did not criticize the use of statistics nor argue for an emphasis on important cases, and he certainly did not cite some professor's views. But he asserted, in his June 13 memorandum, that "some of our people in unnamed offices are not kept busy enough to bolster their morale and to enable them to work under full productivity." In short, Kelley disguised his interest in what later became the quality case program by cloaking it in the language traditionally used by Headquarters when addressing its relations with the field: how to make certain agents are working hard.

2. Office of Planning and Evaluation, FBI Headquarters, memorandum dated May 15, 1975, entitled "A Study of the Use of Personnel."

3. BUAIRTEL from the director of the FBI to all field offices, dated July 12, 1976, entitled "Use of Personnel" (file number 66-19167).

4. Statement of Victor L. Lowe of the General Accounting Office before the Subcommittee on Civil and Constitutional Rights of the House Judiciary Committee (typescript; September 29, 1976), p. 10.

5. U.S. Congress, Senate Committee on Government Operations, Permanent Subcommittee on Investigations, *Federal Narcotics Enforcement: Interim Report*, 94th Cong., 2d sess., 1976, p. 188.

6. U.S. Congress, Senate Committee on Government Operations, Permanent Subcommittee on Investigations, *Federal Drug Enforcement: Hearings*, 94th Cong., 2d sess., 1976, part 5, pp. 1291–303.

7. James Q. Wilson, "The Return of Heroin," *Commentary* (April 1975), pp. 46–50. See also Institute for Defense Analyses, "Trends in Heroin Indicators, January to September, 1974" (December 27, 1974).

8. Mark H. Moore, "Reorganization Plan No. 2 Revisited" (mimeo; Harvard University, John F. Kennedy School of Government, December 31, 1975).

9. Compare my use of subunit concern for autonomy with Crozier's description of subunit concern for power and uncertainty: Michel Crozier, *The Bureaucratic Phenomenon* (Chicago: University of Chicago Press, 1964), chap. 6.

10. Robert K. Merton, "Bureaucratic Structure and Personality," in Merton et al., eds., *Reader in Bureaucracy* (Glencoe, Ill.: Free Press, 1952), pp. 361–71.

Chapter 6

1. Chester I. Barnard, *The Functions of the Executive* (Cambridge, Mass.: Harvard University Press, 1938), p. 215.

2. Herbert Kaufman, *Are Government Organizations Immortal?* (Washington, D.C.: Brookings Institution, 1976), pp. 52–53; *Statistical Abstract of the United States, 1975* (Washington, D.C.: Government Printing Office, 1976), p. 507.

3. To those who argue that public and private administration are essentially the same, I offer the rejoinder of the late Professor Wallace Sayre of Columbia University: public and private administration are alike in all unimportant respects. However fuzzy the line in some borderline cases, the life of a public administrator is distinctive in that he cannot act as if monetary return (profit, sales, equity value) is his chief goal, he cannot act autonomously with respect to arranging and acquiring the factors of production (personnel, buildings, machinery, funds), and he is part of an institutional order that gives legal force to the actions of his organization.

4. Cf. Marver H. Bernstein, *The Job of the Federal Executive* (Washington, D.C.: Brookings Institution, 1958), esp. chap. 2, and Hugh Heclo, *A Government of Strangers: Executive Politics in Washington* (Washington, D.C.: Brookings Institution, 1977).

5. The bureaucrats-as-budget-maximizers theory is most fully developed, but without supporting evidence, in William A. Niskanen, Jr., *Bureaucracy and Representative Government* (Chicago: Aldine-Atherton, 1971), esp. chap. 4.

6. Marc Tipermas, "Jurisdictionalism: The Politics of Executive Reorganization" (Ph.D. diss., Department of Government, Harvard University, 1976).

7. Morton H. Halperin, *Bureaucratic Politics and Foreign Policy* (Washington, D.C.: Brookings Institution, 1974), pp. 51–54.

8. Critical accounts include Sanford J. Ungar, *FBI* (Boston: Atlantic Monthly Press-Little, Brown & Co., 1976), chap. 3, and Ovid Demaris, *The Director* (New York: Harper's Magazine Press, 1975), part 2. Favorable treatments include Ralph de Toledano, *J. Edgar Hoover: The Man and His Time* (New York: Arlington House Manor Books, 1974), chap. 4.

9. Quoted in Ungar, *FBI*, p. 49.

10. Quoted in Toledano, *J. Edgar Hoover*, p. 77.

11. Cf. Toledano, *J. Edgar Hoover*, pp. 95–99; Ungar, *FBI*, pp. 73–74.

12. Toledano, *J. Edgar Hoover*, p. 171.

13. Ungar, *FBI*, p. 57; Joseph Kraft, "J. Edgar Hoover—The Compleat Bureaucrat," *Commentary* (February 1965), p. 60.

14. Ungar, *FBI*, p. 79.

15. John Dean, *Blind Ambition: The White House Years* (New York: Simon and Schuster, 1976), pp. 36–38, and U.S. Congress, Senate Select Committee to Study Government Operations with Respect to Intelligence Activities, *Hearings: The Huston Plan*, 94th Cong., 1st sess., 1975, vol. 2.

16. Victor S. Navasky, *Kennedy Justice* (New York: Atheneum, 1971), chaps. 2, 3.

17. Quoted in Ungar, *FBI*, p. 59.

18. Kraft, "J. Edgar Hoover," p. 59; Ungar, *FBI*, p. 57.

19. Amusing accounts of the minor ways in which FBI agents evaded some Bureau rules are in Joseph L. Schott, *No Left Turns* (New York: Ballantine Books, 1975).

20. U.S. Congress, House Appropriations Subcommittee, *Departments of State, Justice, and Commerce, the Judiciary, and Related Agencies Appropriations for 1973: Hearings*, 92nd Cong., 2d sess., 1972, pp. 54–55, 73. Page numbers are from the FBI reprint of the hearing transcript. Hereafter, *Hearings: 1973 Appropriations* (FBI print).

21. Ibid., p. 12.

22. Ibid.

23. *Hearings: 1977 Appropriations* (FBI print), p. 65.

24. Ibid., p. 63.

25. *Hearings: 1978 Appropriations* (House Committee print), p. 689.

26. Ibid., p. 664.

27. Ungar, *FBI*, p. 140.

28. Comptroller General of the United States, *FBI Domestic Intelligence Operations—Their Purpose and Scope*, a report to the House Committee on the Judiciary (Washington, D.C.: General Accounting Office, February 24, 1976), p. ix.

29. Ibid., pp. 54–55.

30. U.S. Congress, Senate Judiciary Committee, *Hearings on the Nomination of Louis Patrick Gray III, of Connecticut, to be Director, Federal Bureau of Investigation*, 93rd Cong., 1st sess., 1973.

31. U.S. Congress, Senate Judiciary Committee, *Hearings on the Nomination of Clarence M. Kelley, of Missouri, to be Director of the Federal Bureau of Investigation*, 93rd Cong., 1st sess., 1973; Ungar, *FBI*, pp. 144–286; Pat Watters and Stephen Gillers, eds., *Investigating the FBI* (New York: Ballantine Books, 1973); Victor Lasky, *It Didn't Start With Watergate* (New York: Dial Press, 1977); U.S. Congress, Senate Select Committee to Study Government Operations with Respect to Intelligence Activities, *Hearings on the Federal Bureau of Investigation*, 94th Cong., 1st sess., 1975, vol. 6.

32. The list of congressional committees investigating aspects of the FBI is from a list supplied by the director of the FBI.

33. Richard F. Fenno, Jr., *The Power of the Purse* (Boston: Little, Brown & Co., 1966), pp. 368, 374, 384.

34. *Hearings: 1976 Appropriations* (Committee print), pp. 777–876.

35. Cf. David F. Musto, *The American Disease: Origins of Narcotic Control* (New Haven: Yale University Press, 1973), pp. 5–8, 218–21, 244–45.

36. This assumption, in my judgment, is probably wrong for reasons set forth in James Q. Wilson, *Thinking About Crime* (New York: Basic Books, 1975), chap. 7.

37. Edward Jay Epstein, *Agency of Fear* (New York: G. P. Putnam's Sons, 1977), p. 8. The "Plumbers" were a small group of political operatives in the Richard Nixon White House given the task of "stopping the leaks" of sensitive information from the White House and of gathering intelligence about and harassing political opponents.

38. Ibid., chap. 24, esp. p. 201.

39. Ibid., pp. 207, 216, 225.

40. Ibid., p. 252.

41. Ibid., p. 299.

42. Ibid., p. 307.

Chapter 7

1. James Q. Wilson, *Varieties of Police Behavior* (Cambridge, Mass.: Harvard University Press, 1968), chap. 3.

2. Quoted in Sanford J. Ungar, *FBI* (Boston: Atlantic Monthly Press-Little, Brown & Co., 1976), p. 392.

3. Studies attempting to measure the relative importance of personality as opposed to organizational variables on operator behavior include those summarized in Arthur H. Brayfield and Walter H. Crockett, "Employee Attitudes and Employee Performance," *Psychological Bulletin*, vol. 52 (1955), pp. 396–424. On the other hand, there are some studies of police personnel that find relationships between personality variables and various (rather crude) measures of performance. See, for example, Melany E. Baehr et al., "Psychological Assessment of Patrolman Qualifications in Relation to Field Performance," a report to the Law Enforcement Assistance Administration, U.S. Department of Justice (University of Chicago Industrial Relations Center, 1968). In interpreting this evidence, much depends on what one seeks to explain—general patterns of behavior (in which case organizational factors and role definition dominate) or particular conduct toward particular clients (in which case personality factors are likely to be more important).

4. Gresham M. Sykes, *The Society of Captives: A Study of a Maximum Security Prison* (Princeton, N.J.: Princeton University Press, 1958), chap. 2.

5. Wilson, *Varieties of Police Behavior*, chap. 2.

6. The Freedom of Information Act, by providing citizens with access to federal investigative records, may well have the unintended effect of eroding public willingness to give information if citizens believe, rightly or wrongly, that their identity will be divulged to those later seeing agency files.

7. These issues were raised by Mark H. Moore and myself in a memorandum to the attorney general of the United States dated April 1, 1977.

INDEX